Opening the Windows of Blessing

KAY ARTHUR
PETE DE LACY
BOB VEREEN

HARVEST HOUSE™ PUBLISHERS
EUGENE, OREGON

Cover by Koechel Peterson & Associates, Minneapolis, Minnesota

The New Inductive Study Series
OPENING THE WINDOWS OF BLESSING

Published by Harvest House Publishers
Eugene, Oregon 97402
www.harvesthousepublishers.com

Library of Congress Cataloging-in-Publication Data
Arthur, Kay, 1933–
Opening the windows of blessing / Kay Arthur, Pete De Lacy, Bob Vereen.
p. cm. — (The new inductive study series)
ISBN-13: 978-0-7369-0149-9
ISBN-10: 0-7369-0149-3
1. Bible. O.T. Haggai—Study and teaching. 2. Bible. O.T. Zechariah—Study and teaching. 3. Bible. O.T. Malachi—Study and teaching. I. De Lacy, Peter. II. Vereen, Bob. III. Title. IV. Series: Arthur, Kay, 1933–. The new inductive study series.
BS1655.55 .A78 2003
224'.9'0071—dc21 2002010022

Printed in the United States of America

07 08 09 10 11 12 13 14 / BP-KB / 14 13 12 11 10 9 8 7 6 5 4

Contents

How to Get Started...

Let's face it, most of us think that directions are meant to be read only if we can't figure out what to do on our own. Reading directions slows us down and keeps us from getting on with the matter at hand. I understand. I feel the very same way! However, the brief directions which follow are an integral part of your study and will save you time and frustration in the long run, so take a few minutes and begin well!

FIRST

Let's talk about what you are going to need in order to do this study. In addition to this book, you will need three "tools":

1. A Bible. (*The New Inductive Study Bible [NISB]* is *the* ideal Bible for this type of study because of the single-column text, easy-to-read type, high-quality paper, wide margins, and innumerable study helps.) However, no matter which Bible you choose for this study, be aware that you will be instructed to mark its pages. So if you prefer not to mark in your Bible and you have access to a Bible program and a computer, you could print out the text of Haggai, Zechariah, and Malachi and work from your printout. Or you could photocopy the text of these books from your Bible and work on that copy. (This is only permissible *if* it is for your own use.)

2. A four-color ballpoint pen, various colored fine-point pens, colored pencils, or an eight-color Pentel pencil (available from Precept Ministries International or at most office supply stores).

3. A composition book, journal, or notebook for working on your assignments and recording your insights and/or observations. Record your insights chapter by chapter, noting new chapter headings (chapter 1, chapter 2, and so on) as you move through the study.

SECOND

If you are doing this study within the framework of a group and find that you are not able to do each day's study in any given week, simply do what you can. Doing a little is better than doing nothing. Don't be an all-or-nothing person when it comes to Bible study.

Remember that when you get into God's Word, you enter into intensive warfare with the devil (our enemy). In Ephesians 6 we see that every piece of the Christian's spiritual armor relates to the Word of God. Our main offensive weapon is the sword of the Spirit, which Ephesians tells us is the Word of God. Satan wants you to fight with a dull sword. Don't cooperate! You don't have to! Just recognize that it's warfare.

As you study Haggai, Zechariah, and Malachi, you will be given specific instructions for each day. Each assignment will take about 15 to 20 minutes, depending on what is covered that day. Although you will have these specific daily instructions, there are basic things you need to know, do, and remember as you move through the books chapter by chapter. So let's cover these together now.

1. As you read each chapter, train yourself to ask the "5 W's and an H": who, what, when, where, why, and how.

Asking questions like these helps you see exactly what the Word of God is saying. When you interrogate the text with the 5 W's and an H, you'll ask questions like this:

a. **What** is the chapter about?
b. **Who** are the main characters?
c. **When** does this event or teaching take place?
d. **Where** does this happen?
e. **Why** is this being done or said?
f. **How** did it happen?

2. The time references indicating the "when" of events and teachings are very important and should be marked in an easily recognizable way in your Bible. We suggest putting a clock (like the one shown here) in the margin of your Bible beside the verse where the time phrase occurs. You may prefer to draw the clock over the time-related word or phrase, or you may simply want to underline or color the references to time in one specific color.

Remember, time and chronological sequence may be expressed in a number of ways: by mentioning a specific time, day, month, or year, or by mentioning a specific event that clues you in to the time, such as a feast, a year of a king's reign, etc. Time may also be noted by words such as *then, when, afterwards, at this time,* etc.

3. There are key words you will want to color-code in the text of your Bible throughout your study. This is the reason for your colored pencils or pens. Developing the habit of marking your Bible in this way will make a significant difference in the effectiveness of your study and how much you remember.

A **key word** is an important word used by the author repeatedly to convey his message to the reader. In the same way that a key unlocks a door, key words unlock the meaning of the text. Certain key words or phrases will show up throughout the book as a whole, while others will be concentrated in specific chapters or segments of the book. When you color-code a key word, be sure to mark its synonyms in the same way you mark the key word. (Remember that a synonym is a word that has the same meaning in the context as the key word you are marking.) Also mark pronouns that refer to the key word in the same way you are marking the word *(he, him, she, her, it, we, us, our, you, they, them, their).*

Marking key words allows you to identify the word and, thus, the sense of the text easily. You can mark words using colors, symbols, or a combination of both. However, colors are easier to distinguish than symbols when looking back at the text of your Bible. If you use symbols, try to keep them very simple. For example, I mark the word *curse* with a brown cloud outlined in orange **curse**. I mark the word *covenant* in red with a yellow rectangle around it **covenant**.

Color draws your eye quickly to the word and trains it to recognize the word. A symbol conveys the meaning of the word. It may seem a little juvenile to mark words in this way, but if you will get past that feeling and cultivate the habit of marking key words in your Bible in a distinctive and memorable way, you will see a significant difference in your ability to retain what you study.

Let me give you another example of how to mark words. If you want to mark a particular reference to any of the Godhead, you can use yellow for all three, and then to distinguish between the Father, Son, and Holy Spirit, you can draw a distinct symbol for each of the three with a purple pen. You could use a triangle like this: **God** for God, mark the Son with a triangle incorporating a cross in this way: **Jesus**, and mark the Holy Spirit with the triangle incorporating a cloud like this: **Spirit**.

You should devise a color-coding system for marking key words throughout your Bible so that when you look at the pages later, your eye will be drawn to the key words that you've marked. Once you begin color-coding key words, it's easy to forget what symbols or colors you are using to identify a particular word. You may wish to use the bottom portion of the perforated card in the back of this book to write the key words on. Mark the words the way you plan to mark them in your Bible and then use the card as a bookmark. You may want to make one bookmark for words marked consistently throughout your Bible and a different one for each specific book as you study.

In this study course, when you are instructed to mark a key word or phrase, you are given the New American Standard translation of the word or phrase. However, since other translations may translate a particular word or phrase from the Hebrew or Greek into English differently from the NASB, the King James Version (KJV), the New King James Version (NKJV), and the New International Version (NIV) equivalents are referenced in the notes section at the back of this book.

4. Since locations are very important when studying a historical or biographical book of the Bible, you will also want to mark these in a distinguishable way. We suggest simply double-underlining every reference to a location in green (grass and trees are green!).

It is also helpful to look up locations on maps to get a proper perspective of where things are occurring in relationship to each other. Using maps in this way will give you the "geographical" context. If you have a *New Inductive Study Bible* (*NISB*), you will find maps pertinent to a particular passage placed right in the text for ready reference. The maps are included in the Bible text so that you can tell where in the world it happened!

5. Every day when you finish your lesson, meditate on what you saw and ask your heavenly Father how you should live considering the truths you have just seen. At times, depending on how God has spoken to you, you might even want to record these "Lessons for Life" (LFL) in the margin of your Bible by the verses that contain the truth you are applying to your life. Put "LFL" in the margin of your Bible and then as briefly as possible record the lesson for life you want to remember under this heading.

6. Always begin your study with prayer. As you do your part to handle the Word of God accurately, remember that the Bible is a divinely inspired book. The words you are reading are truth, given to you by God that you might know Him and His ways. These truths are divinely revealed.

> For to us God revealed them through the Spirit; for the Spirit searches all things, even the depths of God. For who among men knows the thoughts of a man except the spirit of the man which is in him? Even so the thoughts of God no one knows except the Spirit of God (1 Corinthians 2:10,11).

Therefore, ask God to reveal His truth to you, to lead you and guide you into all truth. He will, if you will ask.

THIRD

This study is designed to encourage you to spend time in the Word of God on a *daily* basis. Since man does not live by bread alone but by every word that comes out of the mouth of God, we each need a daily helping of truth.

The weekly assignments cover all seven days; however, the seventh day is different from the other days. On the seventh day, the focus is on one or more major truths covered in that week's study. You will find a verse or two to memorize and STORE IN YOUR HEART. Then there is a passage to READ AND DISCUSS. This section will be extremely profitable for those who are using this material in a class setting because it will cause the class to focus their attention on a critical portion of Scripture. To aid the individual and/or the class, there's a set of QUESTIONS FOR DISCUSSION OR INDIVIDUAL STUDY. This section is followed with a THOUGHT FOR THE WEEK that will help you understand how to walk in the light of what you've learned.

When you discuss each week's lesson, be sure the answers and insights are supported from the Bible itself rather than opinion or just consensus. Using the Scripture in its context to support your answers develops the habit of "handling the Word accurately." Always examine your insights by carefully observing the text to see what it *says*. Then before you decide the *meaning* of a Scripture or a passage, make sure you interpret it in the light of its context.

Scripture will never contradict Scripture. If it ever seems to be contradictory, you can be assured that somewhere something is being taken out of its context. Therefore, when you come to a passage that is difficult to deal with, reserve your interpretations for a time when you can study the passage in greater depth.

Books in The New Inductive Study Series are survey courses. If you wish to do more in-depth study of a particular book of the Bible, we would suggest using the Precept Upon Precept Bible study course on that book.

More information on Precept Upon Precept Bible studies and where they are being taught can be obtained by contacting Precept Ministries International at 800-763-8280, visiting our website at www.precept.org, or filling out and mailing the response card in the back of this book.

Now then, reading the directions wasn't too bad, was it? You are on your way. Remember the prize is never given to those who don't finish the course... so "hangeth thou in there!"

HAGGAI

Introduction to Haggai

"Obedience" is a word missing from the vocabulary of many people today. Yet it is the key to blessing. When God gave His commandments, statutes, and ordinances to His people, He had one objective—obedience! They were given for their good.

Among those commandments were statutes regarding the Sabbath. God instructed the children of Israel through Moses to observe a Sabbath once they entered the land He planned to give them. Six years the people could sow fields, prune vineyards, and gather crops, but during the seventh year they were commanded to let the land rest—a Sabbath to the Lord (Leviticus 25:1-7).

God warned them that if they chose not to obey, He would punish them seven times for their sins, lay waste their cities, make their sanctuaries desolate, scatter them among nations, and draw out a sword after them (Leviticus 26:27-35). God meant business. If they disobeyed, He would punish them until the land enjoyed its Sabbaths.

At the same time, God promised that if they would humble themselves before Him, confess their iniquity, and make amends, He would remember His covenant with them and not reject or destroy them (Leviticus 26:40-46).

Moses was faithful to give these words to the children of Israel. So they knew what to do, how to do it, and when to do it. But they ignored the words God had spoken. The Lord sent prophet after prophet to remind them of what He had said, but they chose not to listen to His spokesmen. Therefore, God had only one option—to punish them for their own good, for blessing can never come apart from obedience.

Do you realize that because God is God, because He never changes, He deals with us today as He did with the children of Israel? We have His Word—the Bible. We *can* know what God wants us to do and how we are to live so that He might open the windows of heaven and pour out His blessings upon us. No book in the entire Bible illustrates the rewards of obedience and the penalties for disobedience in a more powerful and profound way than the book of Haggai.

Looking Forward to the Future

In all probability, you've heard that wonderful promise God gave to Israel and Judah in Jeremiah 29:11 and you've longed to embrace it as your own. " 'For I know the plans that I have for you,' declares the LORD, 'plans for welfare and not for calamity to give you a future and a hope.' "

Is it applicable to you?

Does God have a plan for your life?

Does God want the best for you?

Does God want you to have a future and a hope?

If so, what's your role in this promise, and how does it affect His ultimate desire for you?

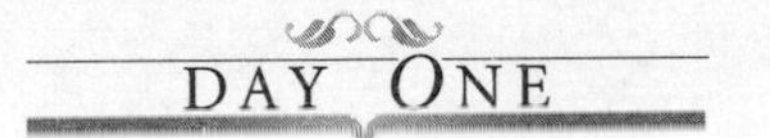

DAY ONE

Having a good grasp on the historical setting of the book of Haggai is critical to understanding the messages this spokesman for God delivered to the discouraged exiles of Judah. It will also help you in your study of Zechariah and Malachi. However, before you begin to establish the historical backdrop, read through this short book to get a sense of what it is all about.

Now, turn your attention to the first verse of chapter one. Using a green marker, underline the time phrase found at the beginning of this verse, including the year, day, and month. Then draw a clock like this in the margin next to verse 1.

Two questions to consider at this point are, Why do you suppose God reveals dates? And what is significant about the date given in verse 1? Does the RULERS AND PROPHETS OF HAGGAI'S TIME chart below give you a clue to the first question?

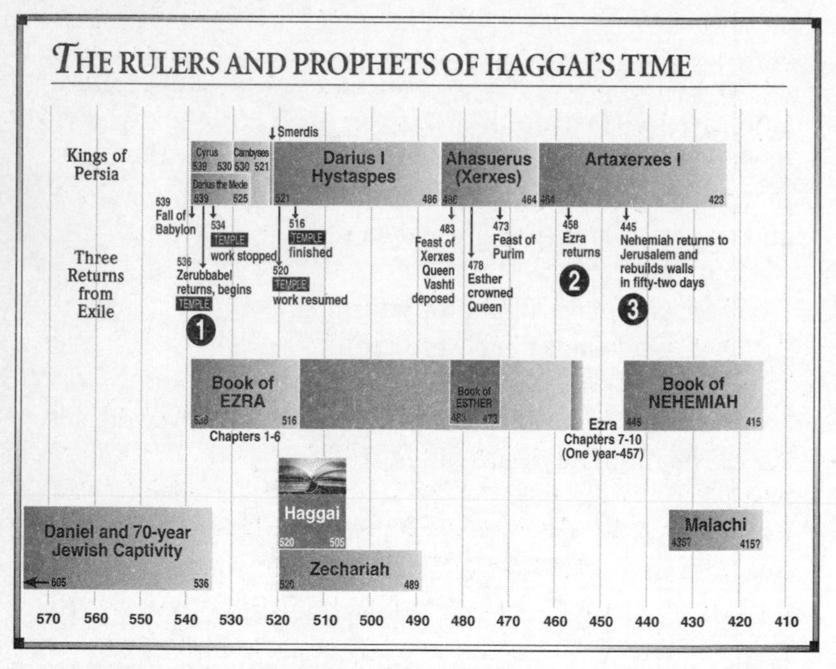

Let's see! Find "Darius I Hystaspes" on the RULERS AND PROPHETS OF HAGGAI'S TIME chart and record the dates he reigned:

Darius I Hystaspes reigned from ______ to ______ B.C.

Now look at the chart and record the dates of Haggai's ministry:

Haggai ministered from ______ to ______ B.C.

From this, what can you conclude about "the second year of Darius the king"? Is this the year Haggai began his ministry?

Why don't you write "520 B.C." in the margin of your Bible next to Haggai 1:1 and record "Haggai begins his ministry" in the appropriate box on the TIME LINE chart on pages 26-27? This chart will be used throughout the week to develop a chronology of events that will help you see the historical setting of the book of Haggai. (If you find this chart too small to record answers, you might want to make a larger one in your notebook.)

DAY TWO

Today we want to answer the second question. What is the significance of 520 B.C. to what God says to the exiles through Haggai?

To answer this question, read 2 Chronicles 36:9-23.

In the *New Inductive Study Bible (NISB)*, 597 B.C. is written in the margin next to verses 9 and 11, 586 B.C. next to verse 18, and 538 B.C. next to verse 22. If you don't have this time-saving tool, write the dates in the margins of your Bible to show the chronology of the corresponding events.

As you read these verses, record the important facts you learn about kings Jehoiachin and Zedekiah, the people of God (Israel), and the temple (the house of the Lord) on the TIME LINE chart (pages 26-27) under the appropriate date.

DAY THREE

Now read Ezra 1:1-3 and notice how similar these verses are to 2 Chronicles 36:22,23.

Some historians believe that Cyrus conquered Babylon in October of 539 B.C. If this is true, "the first year of Cyrus the king of Persia" was from October 539 B.C. through September 538 B.C. These scholars also believe that Cyrus wrote his proclamation in the early months of 538 B.C. (the JEWISH CALENDAR below shows that the first month of the Hebrew calendar corresponds to our March-April). Accordingly, write 538 B.C. in the margin next to Ezra 1:1 to help you see the chronology.

The Jewish Calendar

Babylonian names (B) for the months are still used today for the Jewish calendar. Canaanite names (C) were used prior to the Babylonian captivity in 586 B.C. Four are mentioned in the Old Testament.
Adar-Sheni is an intercalary month used every two to three years or seven times in 19 years.

1st month	2nd month	3rd month	4th month
Nisan (B) Abib (C) March-April	Iyyar (B) Ziv (C) April-May	Sivan (B) May-June	Tammuz (B) June-July
7th month	*8th month*	*9th month*	*10th month*
5th month	**6th month**	**7th month**	**8th month**
Ab (B) July-August	Elul (B) August-September	Tishri (B) Ethanim (C) September-October	Marcheshvan (B) Bul (C) October-November
11th month	*12th month*	*1st month*	*2nd month*
9th month	**10th month**	**11th month**	**12th month**
Chislev (B) November-December	Tebeth (B) December-January	Shebat (B) January-February	Adar (B) February-March
3rd month	*4th month*	*5th month*	*6th month*

Sacred calendar appears in black • Civil calendar appears in gray

Now record the additional information you find in Ezra 1:3 on the TIME LINE chart under the 538 B.C. column.

You probably noticed that in Ezra and 2 Chronicles, one of Jeremiah's prophecies is mentioned. What did he say?

Read Jeremiah 25:1-12. Keep in mind that the prophecy in Jeremiah 25 was given in 605 B.C.—prior to the reign of Jehoiachin and Zedekiah and just before Israel went into Babylonian captivity. Record what you learn in the appropriate column on the TIME LINE chart.

Now read Jeremiah 29:1-14. This prophecy was given after 586 B.C.—when the people of Israel were in exile in

Babylon repaying God for the Sabbaths they owed to the land. Record your insights on the TIME LINE chart under this date.

DAY FOUR

Today, read Isaiah 44:28–45:7 and note what Isaiah the prophet said about a king named Cyrus at least 100 years before his birth.

Look at the RULERS AND PROPHETS OF HAGGAI'S TIME chart once again on page 18 to see when Cyrus and Darius the Mede conquered Babylon.

Now read Ezra 1 to learn what Cyrus did and to see how the people responded. Record the major truths from chapter 1 on your TIME LINE chart under 538 B.C.

Ezra 2 includes a roll call of the first group of people led by Zerubbabel and Joshua (Yeshua) "who came up out of the captivity of the exiles" (2:1) and returned to Jerusalem to rebuild the temple. Look on the RULERS AND PROPHETS OF HAGGAI'S TIME chart to discover the date they returned. Record this fact on the TIME LINE chart under this date.

If you have time to read the entire chapter, it would be a good idea to do so. If not, at least read Ezra 2:64, which gives a summary of the total number of returnees. Add up the total number of people who returned. Record this number on the chart.

How long did it take the first group of exiles to return to Jerusalem from Babylon? The Bible doesn't say. However, read Ezra 7:8,9 to see how long it took the second group of exiles under the leadership of Ezra to make this same journey. Do you think it would have taken

Zerubbabel and Joshua approximately the same amount of time that it took Ezra? Record this also on the TIME LINE chart under 536 B.C.

Finally, read Ezra 3:1 and note where "the sons of Israel" went when they first arrived in the land and then where they later gathered in the seventh month. Now according to what you've already learned in Ezra 1, where were they supposed to go and what were they supposed to do? Did they immediately do it?

DAY FIVE

Read Ezra 3:2-9 to discover what the exiles did once they gathered in Jerusalem. Record these insights in the 536 B.C. column on the TIME LINE chart.

Also, look at the RULERS AND PROPHETS OF HAGGAI'S TIME chart on page 18 to locate the year when the people "began the work" on the temple. You may want to record this date in the margin of your Bible next to verse 8.

Now read Ezra 3:10-13 and record your summary of these events on the TIME LINE chart.

DAY SIX

Read Ezra 4:1-5 and record what you learn on the TIME LINE chart.

Ezra 4:6-23 is parenthetical. These verses tell us how long "the people of the land" tried to discourage "the people of the exile." They tried during "all the days of Cyrus king of Persia, even until the reign of Darius king of Persia" (verse 5). Then they continued during "the reign of

Ahasuerus" (verse 6) and "the days of Artaxerxes" (verses 7-23).

Now read Ezra 4:24. Before you record anything on the chart, look again at the RULERS AND PROPHETS OF HAGGAI'S TIME chart to see when the work on the temple stopped. Record this date on the chart in the margin of your Bible next to verse Ezra 2:4.

Now for your final assignment in Ezra—establishing the historical setting for your studies in Haggai, Zechariah, and Malachi. Read Ezra 5:1,2. Record what you learn about the temple on your chart. Once again, look at the RULERS AND PROPHETS OF HAGGAI'S TIME chart to locate the date when the people "began to rebuild the house of God."

Great! You've finished a good work. Now you have a brief overview of the historical setting of God's people between 605 and 520 B.C. The temple had been lying desolate for some 14 years—from 534 to 520 B.C.—when God raised up the prophets Haggai and Zechariah to speak to His leaders and to His people. What did God say? We'll be looking at the messages delivered by these prophets in the weeks ahead.

DAY SEVEN

Store in your heart: Jeremiah 29:11.

Read and discuss: Jeremiah 25:8-12; 29:5-11; Ezra 1:1-11; 3:1–4:5; 4:24; 5:1,2.

QUESTIONS FOR DISCUSSION OR INDIVIDUAL STUDY

- Using the TIME LINE chart as a guide, what were the major events of each date and in which passage were these truths discovered?

- Why did God punish the children of Israel? What did they do? What did their kings do?
- How long was their punishment? Did the captivity last as long as God said it would? Explain your answer.
- What did God do when the punishment ended? How far in advance did God make plans for ending the captivity?
- How many exiles returned? What did they bring with them when they returned? Where did the resources to pay for the rebuilding of the temple come from?
- When the exiles gathered in Jerusalem, what did they do? Why did they gather in Jerusalem in that specific month? What was celebrated?
- How did enemies in the land respond to their building the temple? What happened shortly after they began?
- What role did Haggai and Zechariah play in the building of the temple?
- What did you learn about God from your study this week? What insights, if any, did you gain into His character or ways?
- Did you gain any insights into the consequences of disobedience? The blessings of obedience?

Thought for the Week

God declared centuries in advance that He would raise up a king to conquer the nation of Israel, take them into captivity, and keep them there for a specific length of time. He also stated that a king would be born to free His chosen people and release them from captivity. God fulfilled His

Word—both events are now recorded in His history book, the Bible.

God did what He said He would do. But His blessing was conditional—based upon the obedience of His people.

It's so easy to get discouraged, frightened, and frustrated. We can become sidetracked with personal projects, business ventures, relationships, finances, recreation, etc. It's easy to have our attention diverted to a thousand other things that have to be done. We often lose our focus and abandon the highest goal—knowing God and living accordingly.

His will and ways become clear to us when studying His Word becomes our first priority. Choosing to study the Bible is the very first act of obedience.

Congratulations! You've made that highest choice—one that pleases God and brings Him glory, for it gives a true estimate of who God is.

TIME LINE

605 B.C.
597 B.C.
586 B.C.

538 B.C.
536 B.C.
534 B.C.
520 B.C.

Do My Circumstances Have Anything to Do with My Behavior?

Have you ever gone through a dry spell—a "drought" in your spiritual life, your marriage, your job, your friendships?

Have you ever struggled with finances? You try to conserve; you try to watch your expenses, but your paycheck just seems to disappear into thin air. The money you thought you had is not there when you need it!

Have you ever invested time, energy, and effort into something that produced fewer results than you thought possible?

What causes this to happen? Does it happen to believers?

Haggai challenged the people of his day who were experiencing these kinds of circumstances to "consider [their] ways"—think about what they were doing.

Is there a relationship between behavior and circumstances?

Haggai answers this question. Let's dig into the text of this short, practical book!

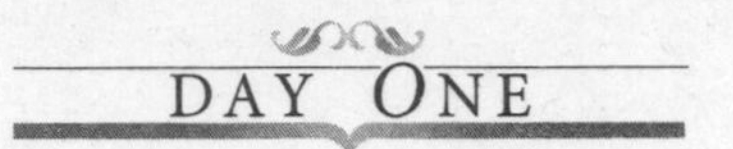

DAY ONE

Last week you read the book of Haggai to get a sense of what the book is all about. You marked the time phrase that appears in 1:1. Today, read through Haggai and mark in the same way any other time phrases that contain specific days, months, and years.

Read Haggai again. This time, using a color other than green, draw a squiggly line under any phrase that refers to the word of the Lord coming by Haggai the prophet or to Haggai speaking by the commission of the Lord.

Review these markings, and you will see that God spoke to Haggai on five different occasions. In your notebook, list these five dates. Record the day, the month, and then the year, if given.

Now look at the JEWISH CALENDAR on page 20. Note the season of the year when each message was given to this farming community. Write out the names of the months next to each date in your notebook.

DAY TWO

Today we'll look at the first message God gave Haggai to proclaim. Read Haggai 1:1-11 and mark each of these key words: *people, the house of the* LORD, *the* LORD *of hosts,* and *consider.* List these key words on the HAGGAI AT A GLANCE chart on page 36. (Remember, in the "How to Get Started" instructions we suggested that you list these key words on the card at the back of this book, mark them distinctively using a different color and/or symbol for each, and then move the bookmark along with you as you go through the book.)

Now read the first two verses of chapter 1 again and record in your notebook whom the first part of this message is directed to and what God said to them through the prophet Haggai.

Read 1:3,4 and record in your notebook to whom the second part of this message is directed.

What charge did God bring against the people?

To connect the teachings of Ezra and Haggai, review Ezra 3:7,8 and answer the following questions:

- What material did the sons of Israel purchase to rebuild the temple? Where was it from?
- From the first four verses of Haggai, what does it appear the people used the wood for?
- What comparison do you see between the people's houses and God's house?

DAY THREE

Read Haggai 1:5-11 one more time and make a list in your notebook of WHAT THE PEOPLE DID. Relate what is being said to the time the message is given.

Make a separate list in your notebook entitled MY JOURNAL ON GOD. From these 11 verses, list things God did and the truths you learn about Him—what He commanded and revealed. Then list how His people responded and the excuses they made. (Leave space at the end for adding truths from the messages that follow.)

Record the main theme of this first message in the appropriate place on the HAGGAI AT A GLANCE chart on page 36. Take a moment to apply what you've learned to your own life. How does what you've learned from Haggai about God and His people relate to your present circumstances—your job, finances, marriage, and personal walk with Him? Record these thoughts in your notebook. Writing will solidify these truths in your memory bank, from which you can draw in times of need.

DAY FOUR

Today, read Haggai 1:12-15 and mark the key words as before.

List in your notebook whom the message is given to and what is said. Record what the people did, when they did it, and how God responded. Add any new insights to your PEOPLE list and your MY JOURNAL ON GOD list.

Record the main thought of this message on the HAGGAI AT A GLANCE chart.

DAY FIVE

According to your study last week of Ezra 4:1-5, you may recall that "...the people of the land *discouraged* the people of Judah, ...*frightened* them from building, and hired counselors against them to *frustrate* their counsel..." (emphasis added). With this in mind, read Haggai 2:1-9, mark the key words, including the words *shake* and *take courage.* Record in your notebook whom the message was written to, when it was given, and its main points.

Continue adding information to the lists you created.

Add the main thought of this message to the HAGGAI AT A GLANCE chart.

Once again, think about how the truths you learned from this message about God and His people apply to you today.

DAY SIX

Read Haggai 2:10-19 marking your key words. Record your observations in your notebook as you did yesterday. Don't forget to continue adding to your PEOPLE list, the JOURNAL ON GOD, and the AT A GLANCE chart.

To conclude this study, read Haggai 2:20-23. Mark and record as you did for the previous four messages.

Review all your notes, the paragraph themes for the five messages, and your JOURNAL ON GOD to conclude what the overall theme of Haggai is. Record this on the HAGGAI AT A GLANCE chart. Fill in any other requested information to complete the chart.

DAY SEVEN

Store in your heart: Haggai 1:8.
Read and discuss: Haggai 1–2.

QUESTIONS FOR DISCUSSION OR INDIVIDUAL STUDY

- What did God tell His people to do when they returned to Jerusalem?
- What did the people of the Exile do that displeased God?
- What did God say He had been doing in response to this behavior?
- What did the people do after Haggai preached God's first rebuke to them?

- How did God respond to their obedience? What did He say to them? Relate this to Ezra 4:1-4. Did their circumstances change due to their change in behavior? Explain your answer.
- What comparison did God make with the former temple? What exhortations did God give the rebuilders? What promises did He make regarding His temple?
- What truths did you learn about God's provision for His work? How does the way God dealt with Israel apply to us today? Do circumstances have anything to do with behavior?
- How did each of the priest's rulings relate to the circumstances and behavior of the people of Israel? What point was God making when using the grain heap and wine vat illustrations? What conclusions did God make regarding their future crops? What caused their promised future circumstances to be different from their past?
- What did you learn about God from your study on Haggai? How do these truths apply to your present circumstances? How do your circumstances relate to your behavior?

Thought for the Week

The children of Israel returned to Jerusalem commanded to rebuild the temple of God. Yet somewhere along the way, they abandoned the task and spent all their energies on the construction of their personal dwelling places using wood purchased for the house of the Lord. God used devastating circumstances to correct their disrespectful behavior.

As we read of the day when God's physical temple will be filled with the wealth of nations and the glory of God, we need to remember there is another temple God desires to fill with His glory today.

In 1 Corinthians 3:16 we read, "Do you not know that you are a temple of God and that the Spirit of God dwells in you? If any man destroys the temple of God, God will destroy him, for the temple of God is holy, and that is what you are."

First Corinthians 6:19 states, "Or do you not know that your body is a temple of the Holy Spirit who is in you, whom you have from God, and that you are not your own? For you have been bought with a price: therefore glorify God in your body."

We are God's temple in today's world. We too are responsible for our personal spiritual development. Paul uses a remodeling term in Romans 12:2: "Be transformed by the *renewing* of your mind." Renewing means taking out something old and putting in something new. To put it another way, as we study the Word of God, the Holy Spirit takes out old thoughts about God (e.g., that He doesn't exist) and replaces them with correct thoughts—truths according to His Word.

We must not give our energies to just the improvement of material things in life—homes, cars, finances, recreation, vocation, hobbies, entertainment, etc. Nor should we use the things intended for God's purposes for our personal benefit and pleasure.

We should, however, constantly be reviewing our priorities, making certain we do not neglect the things of God that strengthen and build us up. Otherwise, we will be discouraged, frightened, or frustrated by the enemies of God. That's why we should continue to make studying His Word a priority.

Haggai at a Glance

Theme of Haggai:

Author:

Historical Setting:

Purpose:

Key Words:

Segment Divisions	Paragraph Themes	Chapter Themes
	1:1-11	1
	1:12-15	
	2:1-9	2
	2:10-19	
	2:20-23	

ZECHARIAH

Introduction to Zechariah

Life is filled with many struggles, disappointments, and setbacks. Sometimes it can feel like it's hard to go on. But in the midst of even our greatest pain, we can always find hope. What greater blessing is there than to have hope when everyone around you is hopeless?

When you hope in the Lord, your hope is secure, an anchor to hold you in the storms of life. He will see you through. The Lord promises blessings, not a curse.

This was the message that came to Zechariah in a time when discouragement and fear gripped the returning exiles, causing them to live in timidity and apathy, without hope.

But God is the God of hope. He is the God who pours out blessing upon those who hope in Him. He is the God who sees and hears and has compassion.

The God of Zechariah does not change. Today, we face terrorists who hate us. Discouragement and fear threaten to rob us of hope and cause us to live in timidity and apathy. But you, beloved, if you hope in God, have the promise of blessing, not a curse.

God always keeps His promises. When He gives us choices and lays the consequences before us, He does what He says He will do. When He makes a covenant, He does not break it. Before the children of Israel entered the land that God had promised them, this truth was declared:

> God is not a man, that He should lie,
> Nor a son of man, that He should repent;
> Has He said, and will He not do it?

> Or has He spoken, and will He not make it good? (Numbers 23:19).

God had kept His promises to Israel and Judah, but they had failed to heed His warnings through the prophets. They had made their choice, so God sent Judah into captivity in Babylon, allowing their holy city, Jerusalem, and their sacred temple, built by Solomon, to be destroyed. But God kept His promise again, eventually allowing them to return.

Ezra and Nehemiah tell of the Jews' return from exile and their reconstruction of the temple, as well as the role of Haggai and Zechariah in stirring up and supporting the rebuilding of the temple. God was faithful to keep His promise, and the temple of the Lord was rebuilt in Jerusalem, with priests ministering the sacrificial system on behalf of the people. Still, the temple and the city lacked their previous glory.

Yet God was not done. He sent His prophets to encourage the people, to show them their future, to give them a reason to hope, to persevere, to press on. God had new blessings He was preparing to bestow upon His people.

Zechariah's message contains promises that God has not yet fulfilled, but we are confident He will keep them because He has kept all the others that He has made—to Israel, to Judah, and to us.

God's word to the discouraged of Zechariah's time was a much needed word, an encouraging word...a word of hope for the future. Let it be such a word to you. Rest in the assurance that God keeps His promises and His message in Zechariah is a message for you...of hope for the future, of encouragement to press on, of blessings God desires to give.

I WILL DWELL IN YOUR MIDST

As God dwelt with Israel in the tabernacle and in Solomon's temple, He now dwells within every believer through the Holy Spirit. How awesome it is to have such a God! Knowing this wonderful truth should have a profound effect on the way we live our lives.

DAY ONE

When you study the Bible, understanding the historical context of a passage is very important to comprehending its message. Since Old Testament prophecy does not exist apart from Old Testament history, understanding how the prophetic books fit into the historical timeline of the Old Testament is vital. Mark the references to time in Zechariah 1:1,7. According to our modern calendar, the second year of Darius' reign was 520 B.C. and the temple was completed in 516 B.C.

Now read Haggai 1:1,15 and 2:1,10,20 to observe when Zechariah's message begins.

Read Ezra 5:1,2 and 6:14,15 to see that Zechariah began his ministry in Ezra's day.

Studying the book of Ezra is a good idea in order to understand the context of Zechariah. If you haven't studied Ezra, read chapters 3–6 of Ezra quickly for an overview of the story.

DAY TWO

Now let's dig into the message of Zechariah. Read Zechariah 1:1-6 and mark the phrase *the word of the LORD came.* Also mark *LORD of Hosts*[1] and *return.* (*Repented* in verse 6 is the same Hebrew word translated *return.*[2] You could mark it in yellow with a red arrow that turns around like this **return** .) Create a bookmark with these key words and phrases listed on it. Mark them on the bookmark in the same way that you will mark them in the text. This will make it easier to be consistent throughout Zechariah. Keep adding to this bookmark as you go through the book. Use it with your daily study.

Note in the margin of your Bible the main message of this first "word of the LORD" through Zechariah.

DAY THREE

Today, read Zechariah 1:7-11, marking *the word of the LORD came* in the same way that you did yesterday. Also continue to mark *LORD of Hosts.* Mark *I saw*[3] and any synonymous references such as *what do you see?,*[4] *the LORD showed me,*[5] and *I lifted up my eyes.*[6] Mark *the angel* (also *the angel who was speaking with me, the angel of the LORD*). Add these to your bookmark.

These verses begin the first of several visions that Zechariah received along with the word of the Lord. In the margin of your Bible, you may want to write "vision" and the basic elements that tell who is involved, what is happening, and where the action occurs.

Zechariah is filled with prophecy—about Messiah, Judah, and the nations. When studying prophecy, note carefully who the prophecy was intended for—the people of that day, you and me, or both!

DAY FOUR

This first vision continues in 1:12-17. Read these verses and continue marking references to the angel who was speaking with Zechariah in his vision. Mark the other words on your bookmark. Add *seventy years,*[7] *Jerusalem, Judah*, and *again*.

Mark *nations*[8] in green with a brown underline. Mark *My house* as a synonym for *temple* by highlighting it in blue. Note in the margin of your Bible the great promise of hope God gives Jerusalem and Zion.

Read verses 18-21. Mark the words from your bookmark. Note any new vision in the margin of your Bible and its main points. Now look over the first chapter and see if you can determine its main subject. Record the main subject or theme (what God is saying in this chapter) in the appropriate space on the ZECHARIAH AT A GLANCE chart on page 84.

You can receive a tremendous blessing from inductive Bible study by keeping a JOURNAL ON GOD—a record of what you learn about God from your study over the years. Begin one now if you have never done this, and add to it daily. What did you learn about God today?

DAY FIVE

Read Zechariah 2, marking the key words on your bookmark. Don't miss the first use of *that day*. This phrase will be used more frequently in chapters 9–14. Note the vision and its main points in the margin of your Bible. List the descriptions of Jerusalem.

Note that in verse 2:10, the Lord begins to speak of coming and dwelling in their midst. See Exodus 29:44-46; 1 Kings 6:12,13; Ezekiel 43:7-9; and Nehemiah 1:8,9, and note where the Lord would dwell.

Read Exodus 40:34,35 and 1 Kings 8:10-13, and observe where the glory of the Lord was in the days of Moses and of Solomon. Then read Ezekiel 10:4,18,19 and 11:22,23. These speak of the temple that was standing in Ezekiel's day, Solomon's temple, which was destroyed by the Babylonians in 586 B.C. Read Ezekiel 43:1-5. This passage speaks of a future time and a future temple.

Read Haggai 2:1-9, where God speaks of a time in the future when the glory of the temple will exceed its former glory.

DAY SIX

Reread Zechariah 2:8-11 carefully and write down who has been sent by the Lord of hosts. Read Luke 2:25-32 and mark *glory*. "Who is the glory of Israel? Read Matthew 16:27,28 and mark *glory*. Who is coming, and when? Who could fulfill the prophecy of coming to dwell in their midst in Zechariah 2:8-11? Don't miss the reference to time in Zechariah 2:11.

Read Ephesians 1:13; 2 Timothy 1:14; and 1 Corinthians 6:19, and make note of where the Holy Spirit dwells.

Now identify the main theme or message of chapter 2 and record it on the ZECHARIAH AT A GLANCE chart.

Day Seven

Store in your heart: Zechariah 1:3.
Read and discuss: Zechariah 1:1-6,12-17; 2:10-13.

Questions for Discussion or Individual Study

- What does God desire for anyone who has strayed from Him?
- What does God promise to do for those who return? By contrast, what happens to those who do not?
- Describe the first vision, recorded in Zechariah 1:7-21.
- In this first vision, what kinds of words did the Lord give to the angel? How do these words affect your hope?
- Describe and discuss the second vision, recorded in Zechariah 2:1-13. To whom are the promises made?
- List several characteristics of God you see in these first two chapters of Zechariah.
- How does knowing God's character help you understand His promises to you? What application can you make to your own situation?
- Where did God dwell in Zechariah's time, and where does He dwell now? What difference should that make in your life?
- What is the glory of the Lord? How does that relate to us today?
- Does this relate to the Second Coming? Explain your answer.

THOUGHT FOR THE WEEK

The fulfillment of God's promises depends upon God's character. He keeps His promises because He is faithful. Yet the specific result can depend on our obedience. We know that we who have believed will stand before the judgment seat of Christ to be judged for the deeds we have done in the body and to receive reward or suffer loss of reward. We know that God blesses obedience and that disobedience has consequences that can extend beyond ourselves.

God calls out to us with comfort and encouragement from His holy Word to excel still more, to press on, to abide in Him.

> The LORD'S lovingkindnesses indeed never cease, for His compassions never fail. They are new every morning; great is Your faithfulness (Lamentations 3:22,23).

We also have a God who is near and not far off. He dwelt among Israel in the tabernacle and then in the temple until the time of the Babylonian captivity. Then, when Jesus was brought to the temple, Simeon declared that He was the glory of Israel. One of the names for Messiah is Immanuel, "God with us." And although Jesus ascended to heaven to sit at the right hand of the Father, He will come again. He has gone to prepare a place for us, and He will come again for us to take us there to be with Him and the Father forever. After He left, Jesus sent the Helper to us so that we would not be left without God's presence with us. Today, God dwells among us in the person of the Holy Spirit, who indwells each and every believer. Think about it! The Almighty, the sovereign Creator of the universe, dwells in you! He has come to be with you and will never leave you. What better source of hope could there be?

CLOTHED IN FESTAL ROBES

Before we were saved, we were much like an orphan in the most despicable and filthy of orphanages. We were clothed in iniquity, in filthy rags, unwashed and unkempt. But when God chose us, the grace of the Lord took away our iniquity and removed our filthy garments. He put clean garments on us, cleansed us by the blood of Christ, and gave us the means to stay clean! As our Father, He expects us to obey Him. His eyes see all, and He says that He will grant us blessings if we walk in His ways. How will we respond to this promise?

DAY ONE

Read Zechariah 3, marking the key words on your bookmark. Describe the vision and its main points in the margin of your Bible.

In this chapter, Joshua is given clean garments. There are other places in Scripture that also speak of clean garments. Read Isaiah 61:1-10; Revelation 3:4,5; and Galatians 3:27. Also compare 2 Peter 3:10-14 and Ephesians 5:25-27. What does it mean to have clean garments?

DAY TWO

In Zechariah 3:6-10, Joshua, the high priest, is admonished about his duties. In the admonishment, the Lord of hosts says that He will send His Branch. To learn more about this Branch, read Isaiah 11–12 and Jeremiah 23:5-8 and 33:14-18. Reread Zechariah 3:7,8 and write in the margin of your Bible who is a symbol of the Branch and who the Branch is.

Also read Romans 15:8-12 and consider possible connections.

Look at the promise in 3:9,10 and mark the time phrase that tells you how long it will take to remove the iniquity from the land (Israel) and what will occur for the people.

Don't forget to write the main subject or theme of chapter 3 on ZECHARIAH AT A GLANCE.

Today, read Zechariah 4, marking the key words on your bookmark. Note who the main character is in this chapter and the main subject or activity—the rebuilding of the temple. Notice what the Lord says about who is involved in both the start and the completion of the temple. What does it mean for the "mountain" to become a plain? Recall the historical context of the rebuilding of the temple that you studied in Haggai. Observe carefully who will be present when the rebuilding starts and is finished. Also note how it is accomplished—by whose power, or whose strength.

Exodus tells of the making of the lampstand that stood in the tabernacle. The tabernacle was a picture of God dwelling with man, and the articles in it pictured various aspects of Jesus. To see this, read John 1:1-9; 8:12; and 9:5.

God is spirit and not flesh, but Scripture often ascribes human characteristics to God—a literary device called anthropomorphism. Zechariah 4 speaks of the eyes of the Lord. Read the following verses and list what the eyes of the Lord see: Deuteronomy 11:11,12; 2 Chronicles 16:7-9; Psalm 34:15,16; Proverbs 5:21; 15:3; and 1 Peter 3:12.

DAY FIVE

The two olive trees are explained as two anointed ones, "which empty the golden oil from themselves." Read Revelation 11:1-12 and compare the accounts.

Revelation 11 speaks of measuring the temple, while Zechariah 2 speaks of measuring Jerusalem. Don't get bogged down in the details you don't understand in this passage from Revelation. (We have also published *Behold, Jesus Is Coming!* a study of Revelation in this New Inductive Study series.) But we must correlate these prophecies.

Zechariah 4:6 is a well-known verse. God will accomplish His plans by His Spirit and His power, not by man's power. Read Haggai 2:4,5,21-23 to see the correlation. Also read Isaiah 30:1,2; 44:1-3; and Ezekiel 36:22-27.

DAY SIX

God prophesies of His Spirit in many places. Read Joel 2:27-29 and Acts 2:1-21 (which quote from and declare the fulfillment of the prophecy in Joel 2).

Record the theme of Zechariah 4 on the appropriate line of the ZECHARIAH AT A GLANCE chart.

DAY SEVEN

Store in your heart: Zechariah 4:6,10.
Read and discuss: Zechariah 3:8; 4:6-8.

QUESTIONS FOR DISCUSSION OR INDIVIDUAL STUDY

- Describe and discuss the first vision, which focused on the clean garments given to Joshua, the high priest.
- What do you learn about Satan in this vision?
- How does this relate to you?
- With whom have you been clothed? What other images of cleansing relate to your salvation?
- From the cross-references you have studied, who is the Branch, and what will He do at His coming?
- Briefly describe what Zechariah sees in chapter 4. What does the angel tell him that these represent?
- Does God really "see" all that happens? What effect should that have on our behavior?
- If God sees all that happens, is there any circumstance or situation that He does not know about? How might this truth affect our confidence in situations that seem "impossible"?
- What relationship should exist between our efforts and God's plans? According to Zechariah 4, what is the role of grace in overcoming obstacles?
- Zerubbabel was the rightful heir to the throne of David. Who places kings in authority? Do human rulers sometimes thwart God's purposes, or are they

part of God's plan for carrying out His purposes? How do you know?

THOUGHT FOR THE WEEK

Joshua and Zerubbabel were the spiritual and temporal heads of Israel. Joshua was the high priest, and Zerubbabel was the leader, the heir to the throne of David. They were to lead the people in restoring the central element of the worship of God of Israel, the temple in Jerusalem. Joshua and the priests would be cleansed of iniquity and set apart for service to God. Faithful service would result in God's favor.

Zerubbabel was to oversee the rebuilding of the temple; he would start it and finish it, but not by his own might or power. Obstacles would be removed, but it would be by God's spirit.

God is omniscient; He knows all things. He is omnipresent; He is everywhere. He is omnipotent; He can do anything. He is Sovereign; He rules over all. Nothing happens that He doesn't see and doesn't know about. No one hides anything from Him, and there is nothing that is out of His control. His plans and purposes cannot be thwarted by any man or any angel, even Satan.

Yet, while we know this to be true of God, we sometimes forget and act as though it were not true. We live as though we were beyond His sight, or as though He were not in control. When circumstances look impossible, very difficult, or beyond our ability, we fail to run to the One who has the power, who is in control, and who is not surprised by what is happening. We try to "fix" things in our own strength—with our talents, our wisdom, our ideas—rather than remembering that it is by His Spirit that we accomplish what He purposed for us.

To live as God has intended in all that we do, we should run to the Father and ask Him for wisdom. Purpose in your heart to do that today. Turn to Him for strength. Rely upon His Spirit. Seek His counsel and rest in His glorious grace.

My House Is Not a Halfway House

Zechariah 6:15 says that "it will take place if you completely obey the LORD your God." God said that those who are far off will come and build the temple of the Lord, but complete obedience is needed from Israel. What happens to us when we don't obey completely? Are our blessings less than what God has in store for us?

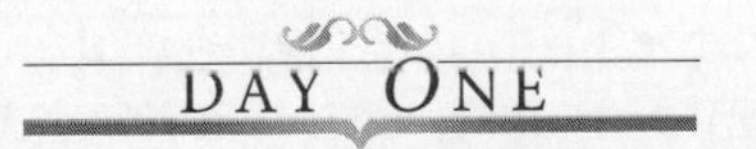

DAY ONE

Read Zechariah 5, marking the key words that you have listed on your bookmark. Don't forget to note the visions in the margin of your Bible.

A "flying" scroll is one that is unrolled for reading, which is why the length is given. An unrolled scroll means that it is clear for all to see; its content is not hidden from view. Note the content of the scroll and then read Ezekiel 2:9–3:11—a passage that should shed some light on understanding the scroll in Zechariah 5.

DAY TWO

According to Zechariah 2:12; 5:3, the land is holy and must be purged or cleansed. Read Exodus 20:7,16; Leviticus

19:11,12; Deuteronomy 27:26; Daniel 12:10; 2 Chronicles 34:5-8; Isaiah 24:5,6; and Jeremiah 16:17,18. These passages should give you insight into the holiness of the land and why it must be purged.

DAY THREE

The second vision of Zechariah 5 involves an "ephah." An ephah is a measure slightly less than a bushel, but here it should be understood as a basket used for measuring. Read Daniel 5, which describes a scene in which the last Babylonian king, Belshazzar, was "weighed" by the Lord (verse 27). Here in Zechariah 5, the ephah is carried out of the land to Shinar, which is in Babylon.

Read Genesis 11:1-9 and Daniel 1:1,2. Shinar is an actual place in the historical country of Babylon, yet it is also used metaphorically to speak of wickedness in general. Read Zechariah 2:7; Revelation 17:1-5; 18:1,2,21; and Jeremiah 51:1-9 to gain insight on the wickedness of Israel and the role of Babylon.

Don't forget to record the theme of chapter 5 on the ZECHARIAH AT A GLANCE chart.

DAY FOUR

Read Zechariah 6, marking key words and phrases.

Compare the vision of Zechariah 6:1-8 with the visions of Zechariah 1:7-11 and Revelation 6:1-8. Note that the chariots come from between two mountains—from a valley. For another prophetic reference to a valley of judgment, read Joel 3:1,2,12-14.

Zechariah 2:6; Jeremiah 49:36; Ezekiel 37:9; and Revelation 7:1 all speak of the four winds or spirits of heaven. The Hebrew word *ruach* can be translated "breath," "wind," or "spirit," so these could be references to angels or physical winds.

The horses in the vision of Zechariah 6:1-8 patrol the north and south. Israel's enemies of that day always came from the north or south because the Mediterranean Sea was to the west, and the desert bordered them to the east. For an example of enemies coming from the north and south, read Daniel 11.

DAY FIVE

Zechariah 6:9 begins another message from the Lord concerning Joshua, the high priest. But that message also includes another prophecy concerning the Branch. Read Zechariah 6:9-15 again, and then read Isaiah 4:2; Jeremiah 23:5,6; 33:15-18; and Zechariah 3:8-10. List what you learn about the Branch.

DAY SIX

List all you learn about the crown given to Joshua in Zechariah 6:11. There are two kinds of crowns in the Old Testament. The one in this vision is not the crown of the high priest but of rulers. Note that Joshua, the high priest, is given a royal crown. Note who will rebuild the temple of the Lord, who will sit and rule, and who will be a priest. Compare with Zechariah 3:8-10 again. Observe what the text says that Joshua and his friends are to be and what the crown on Joshua is in 6:14.

The Babylonians had taken all the valuables from the temple when God's people were taken into captivity. But upon the return of the remnant of Judah, God restored their fortunes. Read Ezra 1:1-11; 7:14-16; 8:26-30; and Jeremiah 28:6 for a description of the wealth that was returned to Judah and was contributed for the rebuilding of the temple. Just as Israel had come out of Egypt with great wealth, so the return from exile in Babylon was accompanied by great wealth.

Summarize Zechariah 6 on your ZECHARIAH AT A GLANCE chart. What were the main topics or subjects covered?

DAY SEVEN

Store in your heart: 1 Peter 4:17.

Read and discuss: Zechariah 5:1-11; 6:9-15; 1 Peter 4:17; Titus 2:11-14.

QUESTIONS FOR DISCUSSION OR INDIVIDUAL STUDY

- Briefly review the content of the two visions of Zechariah 5:1-11. What did you learn from Ezekiel about scrolls?
- From the cross-references in Day Two (Exodus 20:7,16; Leviticus 19:11,12; Deuteronomy 27:26; Daniel 12:10; 2 Chronicles 34:5-8; Isaiah 24:5,6; and Jeremiah 16:17,18), what did you learn about the Lord's attitude toward sin among mankind? What must be done with sin?
- What is the Lord's attitude toward sin in the land of Israel? Why?

- How does Israel's example affect us? What lesson should we take for ourselves from God's dealings with Israel?
- Describe the vision in Zechariah 6:1-8.
- What is the main point of the vision of the horses and chariots in Zechariah 6:1-8?
- Who are the enemies of God? Where do they dwell? Who will defeat them and establish peace on the earth?
- Discuss the content of the vision about the crown in Zechariah 6:9-15.
- What principles can we learn from the offerings given to make the crown for Joshua?
- From your studies so far in Zechariah, who do you think is the Branch? How does the Branch relate to the high priest and the king?
- God restored the fortunes of those held captive in Babylon. What does this imply for people today who are released from captivity in the kingdom of darkness? What kinds of riches will the Lord give them?

THOUGHT FOR THE WEEK

God judges sin. The flying scroll detailed the curse for those who steal and swear. Wickedness would have its own temple in Babylon. God would judge Israel for her sin by carrying her away in exile to Babylon. Yet there would be a temple of the Lord in Israel again, built by the Branch, who would rule and be a priest.

God is holy. He has declared that we are a holy people, a royal priesthood, and He commands us to be holy even as He is holy. Because of His holiness, He must judge sin. Throughout the Old Testament, God instilled in His people His own standard of holiness so that they could approach Him. He is Holy, so His people and His land were to be holy. Therefore, they must purify, purge, and cleanse themselves and the land.

As Christians, we are chosen to be pure and holy before Him. We are to be cleansed by the washing of water with the Word, spotless and blameless at His coming, so that we will not have to endure the judgment that is coming. When we stand before the judgment seat of Christ, let us be found holy.

This holy God is also the Lord of the whole earth. He rules over all; He is sovereign. He establishes kings to rule over kingdoms on earth, and He establishes the King who will rule over the kingdom of heaven. Revelation describes the coming King, who is King of kings and Lord of lords and who will rule and reign forever. One day, all those who have sat on thrones and worn a crown will bow to Him.

Just as the earthly priests and rulers served as earthly reminders of the heavenly, so the tabernacle on earth was a reminder of the heavenly tabernacle and the earthly Sabbath is a reminder of the heavenly Sabbath. The earthly points the way to the heavenly. But the perfection of the heavenly contrasts with the imperfection of the earthly.

Zerubbabel and Joshua worked to build the earthly temple, but He who is coming—the true King and true High Priest—will Himself build the true temple. Come, Lord Jesus! Come Thou fount of every blessing!

Blessing Others

Israel's mourning will be turned to gladness. Once taken into captivity because of their sin, they will return and dwell in joy. God's people are to be a blessing among the nations, but how can we be a blessing when we turn a blind eye or a stubborn shoulder to God's Word or devise evil in our hearts?

DAY ONE

Note the time phrase in Zechariah 7:1 and compare it to Zechariah 1:1 and the time phrases in Haggai. Then read all of Zechariah 7, marking the key words and phrases.

Note the question the representatives from Bethel asked and the question the Lord directed back to them. Their attitude in worship had not been right. The "former prophets" included all the prophets up through Jeremiah.

DAY TWO

The festival cycle of Israel is outlined best in Leviticus 23. Fasting was included as an act of worshiping the holy God. But the fasts mentioned in Zechariah are not the result of God's direct commands. Instead, they are traditions associated with the destruction of Jerusalem and the temple.

The question the people asked in the time of Zechariah was, Should we still mourn the destruction of Solomon's temple now that the temple is being rebuilt?

Read 2 Kings 25:1-12,22-26 for an account of events commemorated by the fasts mentioned in Zechariah 7.

The fasting and mourning of the fifth month was on the ninth of Av and was instituted in memory of the destruction of the temple in 586 B.C., as recorded in 2 Kings 25:9.

The fasting and mourning of the seventh month is not associated with the Day of Atonement, as it is in Leviticus 23, but is in remembrance of the murder of Gedaliah, who had been appointed governor by the Babylonians (this story is found in 2 Kings 25:22-25). This fast came on the third of Tishri, right after the celebration of the New Year, Rosh Hashanah.

For examples of genuine fasting and mourning, read Ezra 10:1-6; Daniel 10:1-3; and Joel 2:12-19.

Zechariah 8:19 mentions the fasts of the fourth, fifth, seventh, and tenth months.

The fast of the fourth month commemorated Jerusalem's defeat on the ninth day of the month by Nebuchadnezzar, as recorded in 2 Kings 25:3,4. Later in Jewish history, Jerusalem was taken on the seventeenth day by the Roman general Titus, and that destruction is also remembered in the fast of the fourth month. Today that fast is held on the seventeenth day of Tammuz, the fourth month of the Jewish year.

The fast of the tenth month commemorated the beginning of the siege of Jerusalem on the tenth day (2 Kings 25:1).

DAY THREE

Preserving justice for widows, orphans, strangers, and the poor was a basic commandment of the Lord. Read Exodus 22:21-27 and Deuteronomy 24:17-21 and 27:19. Yet God's people had not practiced this from the heart. (Read Jeremiah 7:3-11; Malachi 3:5; and Luke 11:42). They had made their hearts like flint. Hard-heartedness afflicted Israel. Read Deuteronomy 15:7-11 and Proverbs 28:14.

Hard-heartedness should not afflict Christians. Read Mark 8:14-21; Ephesians 4:17-19; Hebrews 3:8-19; and 1 John 3:10,17,18.

Don't forget to add the theme of chapter 7 to your ZECHARIAH AT A GLANCE chart.

DAY FOUR

Read Zechariah 8 and mark the key words and phrases from your bookmark. For this chapter, be sure to mark *save* and *remnant*[9] as a key word.

From Zechariah 8:1-8, write out the description of Jerusalem as it will be after the Lord's return. Consider what that meant to those living in Jerusalem at the time of Zechariah's message. Also describe God's relationship with Israel (Zion) and what He intends to do for Israel.

DAY FIVE

Read Zechariah 8:9-13 and list what the people are to do. Continue making a list of how God relates to Israel and what He intends to do for them. Note the contrast between what was "before," what is "now," and what the future will be.

Zechariah 8:14-17 gives a comparison and contrast of God's purposes or intentions. Make a note of them in the margin of your Bible. Add to your list of the things the people are to do.

DAY SIX

Read Jeremiah 31:1-14.

Zechariah 8:20 continues the theme of the promise of future blessing in Israel and adds an additional note. Read Zechariah 8:20-23 and note who will go up to Jerusalem to entreat the favor of the Lord. Also note how the nations will relate to the Jewish people in that day.

Read Genesis 12:1-3 and consider God's intention for those who bless Abraham's offspring (Israel) and for those who curse them.

Add the theme of chapter 8 to ZECHARIAH AT A GLANCE chart.

DAY SEVEN

Store in your heart: Zechariah 7:9,10.
Read and discuss: Zechariah 7:9-14; 8:9-19.

QUESTIONS FOR DISCUSSION OR INDIVIDUAL STUDY

- Discuss what Zechariah 7 teaches about the purpose of fasting and mourning. What does God say that Israel had failed to do?

- What is the difference between presenting sacrifices and offerings for yourself, and presenting sacrifices and offerings for God?

- In what ways can we demonstrate our love for God today? Are physical acts the only way we demonstrate our love?
- If we "turn a deaf ear" to the Lord, can we expect Him to hear our prayers? Can we expect Him to continue speaking to us?
- How does God act if we refuse to pay attention to Him and are stubborn or "deaf"?
- What led up to God's judgment of Israel?
- Discuss God's return to Zion in Zechariah 8. Describe what life in Jerusalem will be like in that day.
- Does God's return depend upon Israel's change of behavior or on God's character?
- Did God change His mind, or was His promise of restoration something He had determined beforehand?
- According to Zechariah 8, what kind of behavior does God expect?
- After God returns to Zion, how will Israel relate to other nations?
- What does Israel's relationship to God teach us about our relationship to God?
- Is there anything in this chapter about Gentiles and their relationship to the Jews?

THOUGHT FOR THE WEEK

Fasting—eating certain foods or none at all—can be done for the right reasons or for the wrong reasons. The men of Bethel sought to know from the Lord what customs they should keep now that they were back in the land. The Lord had a simple answer: Who are you fasting for? Examine your motive.

The quality of a person's relationship with God is determined by the condition of his or her heart. Our behavior is a reflection of our heart. A heart that is hard as stone needs to be softened, and that is what God does in the new covenant. Then we are able to love and be loved.

Sacrifices and offerings were always intended to indicate a heart relationship with God. But today, as they did in Zechariah's time, people perform acts of ritual obedience without a heart that belongs to God.

Obedience *follows* a changed heart. Only with a changed heart can we love our brother; bring justice for the widow, the orphan, and the poor; and truly love God. Only with a changed heart can we be a blessing to others. He first loved us that we might love Him. He has blessed us that we might bless others.

"Great is Thy faithfulness, O God my Father; ...Morning by morning new mercies I see." Imagine the hymns of praise the people of Israel will sing upon fulfillment of the promises God gives in these passages. All of Israel's past and present sorrows will be forgotten. The night will be dispelled; the dawn will break anew.

How very much like Easter that will be for Israel. In that day they will again have the favor of the Lord in all its glory. The promise of Messiah, the promise of full restoration in Israel, and the promise of a future of blessing and hope in the land—all the nations will see the favor of the Lord upon Israel. Israel's future is brighter than the past or present.

YOUR KING IS COMING

A day is coming when we will not struggle under the yoke of oppression. Hope will become reality when the King comes again. He will bring justice, save His people, and strengthen them. Then they will walk in obedience. If God has saved and strengthened you, then you, too, can walk in obedience.

DAY ONE

Read Zechariah 9 and mark the key words and phrases. This chapter is the start of a new segment, so note the opening phrase of the chapter. Add *covenant* and *king* to your bookmark, and continue marking these through the rest of the book. You should have marked *in that day* in chapter 2. Mark it in chapters 9–14 as well.

Double underline in green the cities that are mentioned in Zechariah 9:1-8. Ashkelon, Gaza, Ekron, and Ashdod were Philistine cities. Note the fate of every place mentioned other than Jerusalem.

DAY TWO

Zechariah 9:9-10 includes another messianic prophecy. Read Zechariah 2:10; Matthew 21:1-11; and John 12:12-16, and compare these passages to Zechariah 9:9.

DAY THREE

Read Zechariah 8:13 and 9:11-17. Then read Jeremiah 23:5-8; 30:10,11; 31:7-14; 46:27,28; and Romans 9:27 and 11:25-27. Because of His covenant, what does God promise to do for Israel?

Summarize Zechariah 9, and add your summary to your ZECHARIAH AT A GLANCE chart.

DAY FOUR

Read Zechariah 10, marking the key words and phrases. Add *shepherd* to your bookmark. For this chapter, mark *I will strengthen,* and determine whom God will strengthen. Also underline geographical references.

DAY FIVE

Describe the condition of the people in Zechariah 10:1,2. Compare Zechariah 10:3 with 2 Samuel 5:1,2; 1 Kings 22:17; and Ezekiel 34:1-10. Who are the shepherds?

DAY SIX

Read Zechariah 10:3b-12 ("3b" refers to the last clause in verse 3, starting with "For the LORD of hosts"). List what the Lord will do for His people and what they will be like.

Add the theme of Zechariah 10 to the ZECHARIAH AT A GLANCE chart.

DAY SEVEN

Store in your heart: Zechariah 9:9.
Read and discuss: Zechariah 9:11-17; 10:3b-12.

QUESTIONS FOR DISCUSSION OR INDIVIDUAL STUDY

- Who is the one mounted on a donkey in Zechariah 9:9? Has this already happened, or is it still in the future? How do you know?
- What does it mean to "cut off the chariot…and the bow of war" (Zechariah 9:10)? How are these related to the One who comes mounted on a donkey?
- When do the events of Zechariah 9:11–10:12 occur?
- What does the Lord of hosts promise to do for Israel?
- What does the Lord of hosts promise for other nations or cities?
- What is the basis for the Lord's different promises?
- Does the Lord promise anything different for you as a child of God, or will you be treated the same as everyone else?

THOUGHT FOR THE WEEK

Israel's expectations were for a Messiah who would throw off the yoke of Roman rule, a warrior, as Zechariah 9 proclaims. Their king would come, just and endowed with salvation. The Lord would gather Israel, restore them and strengthen them, and their hearts would rejoice. Because of covenant.

"Because of the blood of My covenant" (Zechariah 9:11) is one of the most powerful phrases in the Bible. It is the basis for God's actions toward His covenant partners. God made covenant promises to Israel that He has already kept, and He intends to keep others in the future. He promised a King who would come on a donkey, and He fulfilled that promise as our Lord Jesus Christ rode into Jerusalem the week before His crucifixion. Israel's expectations were for a Messiah who would throw off the yoke of Roman rule, the warrior proclaimed in Zechariah 9. But the Prince of Peace came at that time not to establish peace on earth—in the sense of the end of war—but to make peace with God possible.

He will come again as a warrior and judge. Then Israel will look upon Him whom they have pierced, and all Israel will believe. The promise of His coming again is as certain as His first coming because it is founded upon God's covenant.

So, too, He has made covenant promises to those who have believed in His Son, Jesus, and have entered into the new covenant with Him.

The fulfillment of God's covenant promises rests not on our behavior but on the character of God. He is faithful, even if we are faithless. How comforting it is to know that the security of our salvation rests in God, who is faithful to His covenant promises. Praise Him for His faithfulness.

The faithful fulfillment of God's covenant promises is a blessing for us to look forward to with the utmost assurance. For though the blessing might not be ours today, we have the certainty of its coming.

We have God's Word on it.

The Blessing of the Lord as My Shepherd

Shepherds have an important job, and if they don't do it properly, their sheep will be scattered and perish. Someone must seek them and restore them to health in order to save them. Even though some earthly shepherds have been found faithless, God is faithful. We have the Good Shepherd to guard us and care for us.

DAY ONE

Read and mark Zechariah 11.

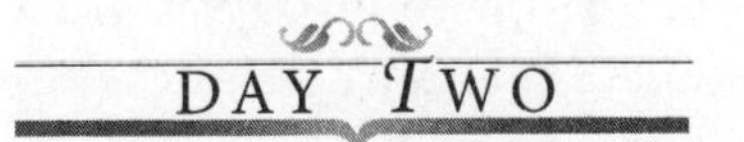

DAY TWO

Zechariah 9–11 focuses on judgment. Zechariah 9:1–11:3 speaks of the judgment of the nations. In Zechariah 11:4, the prophecy returns to Israel. Read Zechariah 11:4-17 again, and mark or note the use of *flock*. You should have already marked *shepherd*. Think about who the flock is and who the shepherds might be.

DAY THREE

Read John 10:1-16,24-28; 21:15-17; and Acts 20:28-30. These Scriptures give New Testament insight into the shepherd and his flock. Compare what you learn from these Scriptures to Zechariah 11.

DAY FOUR

Read Zechariah 11:7-17 again, marking *Favor* and *Union.* Then read 1 Kings 12:1-19. Is Zechariah 11:7-17 referring back in time to Rehoboam—is this when Favor and Union were broken? Or does Zechariah point forward in time, to some event after Zechariah's time?

Don't forget to summarize the message of Zechariah 11 and add it to the ZECHARIAH AT A GLANCE chart.

DAY FIVE

Read and mark Zechariah 12. Don't miss *Jerusalem* and the phrases *The burden of the word of the LORD concerning Israel* and *the Spirit of grace.* Mark *Spirit* like this: Spirit in purple and color the inside in yellow.

DAY SIX

List all the things in Zechariah 12 that God said He will do "in that day." There is a great contrast in this chapter between what God will do with the nations and what He will do with Israel. On your list, make that contrast clear. (You might want to make two separate lists.)

DAY SEVEN

Store in your heart: Zechariah 12:10.

Read and discuss: Zechariah 11:4-17. Note the contrast with Zechariah 12.

QUESTIONS FOR DISCUSSION OR INDIVIDUAL STUDY

- Discuss what you learned from your study of Zechariah 11 and the New Testament cross-references about sheep and shepherds (John 10:1-16,24-28; 21:15-17; Acts 20:28-30).
- How had God shepherded Israel? What does it mean that Zechariah had a staff named Favor and a staff named Union?
- What does it mean that Zechariah broke Favor and Union?
- Who are the shepherds who would be raised up but would not care for the flock?
- Discuss the change in Zechariah 12 regarding God's attitude toward Israel. How does it relate to shepherding?

THOUGHT FOR THE WEEK

When David was a shepherd, he defended his sheep from the lion and the bear. Yet he knew the Lord was his shepherd. Israel has a Shepherd who will defend them "in that day" from all enemies. He will rescue them from those who seek to destroy them, and He will lead them in victory.

Almost everyone is familiar with Psalm 23. It's often quoted at funerals and other difficult times to give comfort to those who are hurting. Many have even committed it to memory so they can always be reminded of God's care. The metaphor of the shepherd and his flock is an important one for every Christian to understand because our Shepherd is the only perfect one and our relationship to Him is so wonderfully described in the Scriptures.

If we fully grasp this metaphor, we come face-to-face with our position as sheep. We are reminded of our utter helplessness and our total dependence upon the Shepherd. We are delivered from the illusion that we can do things on our own when we realize that we are only sheep. All the strength and blessings we need come from the Shepherd.

They Will Look upon Me Whom They Have Pierced

Our hope is coming! "In that day," declares the Lord, grace will be poured out. A remnant will be saved, and they will be His people. God has promised that one day Israel will see and believe. This hasn't happened yet to Israel as a nation, but what about you? Have you seen and believed?

DAY ONE

Read Zechariah 12 again. Who does the "Me" refer to in verse 10? Read John 19:37. If you need more context, read John 19:17-42. Also read Matthew 24:30 and Revelation 1:7. Then decide whether the prophecy in Zechariah 12:10 has already been fulfilled or is yet to come.

DAY TWO

Read Isaiah 44:3; Ezekiel 39:29; and Joel 2:28,29. These speak of the Spirit being poured out on Israel. Acts 2:17-21 declares the fulfillment of Joel 2, but note that in Zechariah 12:10, the house of David and the inhabitants of Jerusalem look upon the One they have pierced and they mourn.

DAY THREE

Read Ezra 9:8; Psalm 45:2; 84:11; Proverbs 3:34; 4:9; Jeremiah 31:2; and Zechariah 4:7 and 12:10. All these passages mention grace. What is the Old Testament concept of grace?

DAY FOUR

Compare the use of the words "pierce," "wound," and "strike" in Zechariah 12:10; 13:6,7; and Matthew 26:31. Summarize the theme of Zechariah 12 and add it to your ZECHARIAH AT A GLANCE chart.

DAY FIVE

Read and mark Zechariah 13. Mark *third, third part,* and their pronouns the same way you marked *remnant.* Note the use of *Shepherd* in Zechariah 13:7. List what you learn by marking *shepherd* in this chapter. Review what you saw in Zechariah 11 about shepherds. Who is the shepherd, and to what is Jesus referring prophetically in Matthew 26:31?

DAY SIX

Zechariah 13:8,9 mentions the "third" or "third part." Reread Zechariah 8:6-12. Also read Micah 2:12 and Jeremiah 23:1-6. Read Romans 9:27 and 11:26-31. If you have time, read 2 Peter 3:1-10.

Review Zechariah 12–13 and outline what will happen "in that day." Then add your summary of the theme of Zechariah 13 to your ZECHARIAH AT A GLANCE chart.

DAY SEVEN

Store in your heart: Zechariah 13:7.
Read and discuss: Zechariah 12–13.

QUESTIONS FOR DISCUSSION OR INDIVIDUAL STUDY

- Contrast the use of the word "shepherd" in Zechariah 11 and Zechariah 12–13.
- What did you learn from the list you made from Zechariah 12–13 about what will happen "in that day"?
- When Messiah comes again, will Israel recognize Him as the one whom they crucified?
- List the names associated with Messiah in Zechariah (Shepherd, Associate, Branch, etc.). Discuss their significance.
- How does the concept of grace fit into Zechariah?
- Neither "faith" nor "believe" are mentioned in Zechariah, but "save" and "saved" are mentioned. According to Psalm 145:18,19, how will Israel be saved?
- Sometimes we are impatient for the Lord to come. Should we be impatient? If we are, is it because we have a heart for the lost or because our motives are selfish and we wish our present circumstances would end?

THOUGHT FOR THE WEEK

"In that day" the Lord would watch over Judah. He would open a fountain for the house of David and for Jerusalem for sin and impurity. They would be refined and purified, and only one third would come through the fire. But those who survive would call on the name of the Lord and be His people.

Jerusalem would be a heavy stone for the nations; God would fight for His people Israel and for Jerusalem. All peoples of all nations who would come against Jerusalem would be detroyed, but on Jerusalem, would be blessing.

> God, being rich in mercy, because of His great love with which He loved us, even when we were dead in our transgressions, made us alive together with Christ (by grace you have been saved), and raised us up with Him, and seated us with Him in the heavenly places in Christ Jesus, so that in the ages to come He might show the surpassing riches of His grace in kindness toward us in Christ Jesus. For by grace you have been saved through faith; and that not of yourselves, it is the gift of God (Ephesians 2:4-8).

What a glorious truth—God is gracious toward us. But God is also gracious toward Israel, for a remnant will be saved. Those who see Messiah when He comes will believe and will be saved—by grace, not the Law.

Salvation has always been by grace through faith in the promised Messiah. Abraham believed, and it was counted as righteousness. The Law was added because of our transgressions, but salvation has always been according to the promise, by faith.

But when Jesus came to Israel riding on a donkey, the Jews did not recognize Him and believe. Instead, they crucified Him. They still do not believe that the Messiah has come, and they wait for His appearing. But for those who have believed in Jesus—Jew and Gentile—Messiah has come, and He will come again. We wait for Him. But how do we wait?

While God's Word tells us to be alert for His coming, it is easy to forget that God's timing is according to His plan and purposes, and it has to do with the salvation of the lost. In our own present circumstances, if we look to the Lord's return to relieve us of our suffering, do we think with the mind of Christ? Or do we have a heart for evangelizing the lost, that they may receive eternal life? Where is our focus? We must remember God's love and remain focused on His mercy and grace toward us and all sinners.

THE NATIONS WILL WORSHIP THE KING

What wonderful blessings are in store for those believers who will see the return of the King. But it will not be such a blessing for those who refuse to believe and acknowledge Him. "In that day" those who worship the King will have rain and those who will not worship the King will have no rain but will be smitten with a plague from the Lord. Obedience will bring blessing in that day, and disobedience will bring a curse. In these days of waiting, let us show our allegiance through our obedience and worship the coming King. Then will He open up the windows of blessing.

DAY ONE

Read Zechariah 14 and mark the key words and phrases.

DAY TWO

Zechariah 14 speaks of a great battle. List or draw on a time line the sequence of events in this chapter.

Add the theme of Zechariah 14 to your ZECHARIAH AT A GLANCE chart. Then summarize the overall message of the book and record it in the chart.

DAY THREE

Read Revelation 16:12-19 and 19:11-21. Armageddon is almost universally known as the final battle at the end of the world. What does the Bible say about Armageddon (or as the NASB puts it, Har-Magedon)? Where are the armies gathered, and where do they fight?

DAY FOUR

Read Isaiah 63:1-6; Joel 3:9-15; and Revelation 14:14-20 and 19:15. See how these relate to the battle described in Zechariah 14.

Mark and then list everything you learn about Jerusalem in Zechariah 14.

DAY FIVE

Read Leviticus 23:34-43 and Deuteronomy 16:13-16 and 31:10,11 for background on Zechariah 14:16-19 and the Feast of Booths. The Feast of Booths was celebrated in conjunction with the Feast of Trumpets and the Day of Atonement.

DAY SIX

One of the final phrases in Zechariah is "HOLY TO THE LORD" (14:20). It was inscribed on a plate on the headband of the high priest. Many things were dedicated as "holy to the Lord" under the Law. See the last time "holy to the Lord" is used in the Bible—Luke 2:21-38. To be "holy to the Lord" is to be set apart for Him, to be pure, without spot or blemish or stain of sin. Read 2 Peter 3:14 and let that be your desire.

DAY SEVEN

Store in your heart: Zechariah 14:4.
Read and discuss: Zechariah 14.

QUESTIONS FOR DISCUSSION OR INDIVIDUAL STUDY

- Review the sequence of events in Zechariah 14.
- Discuss everything that happens with respect to Jerusalem.
- Much of the world has heard about Armageddon. How does the biblical account match the world's view? How does it differ?
- What is the purpose of the great war that begins with the gathering of a vast army at the plain of Megiddo? Is it the "end of the world" or something else?
- How does God's character relate to this great conflict?
- How should we think of this battle? Does it affect us in any way?
- What does it mean to be "holy to the Lord"?
- Reflect on your own personal holiness. Are you "holy to the Lord?" Do you want to be? What needs to change in your life?

THOUGHT FOR THE WEEK

The Lord will come to Jerusalem "in that day" and stand on the Mount of Olives. It will be a day unlike any other. There will be panic, plague, and battle among the nations who gather against Jerusalem. But there will be peace, security, celebration, and feasts for those who worship the Lord of Hosts.

The bells of the horses will be inscribed, "Holy to the Lord." Every cooking pot in Jerusalem and in Judah will be holy to the Lord of Hosts. The bottom line of Zechariah is that there is a day coming when the Lord will be seen as holy. There is a day coming when Israel and Jerusalem will be restored to their former status and will be a blessing to the nations.

Every believer should pursue holiness with his or her whole heart. Being "holy to the Lord" should be the goal of every person. The ultimate purpose of the Bible is to teach us how to be "holy to the Lord." In every book of the Bible, God reveals Himself and calls us to be like His Son, Jesus, who is holy. Someday, when we receive our glorified body and are present with the Lord in heaven, we will be as holy as we will ever be. Then we will stand (or perhaps fall on our faces in worship) in the presence of the perfect Holiness, God Himself.

And one day, the present heavens and earth will be destroyed and a new heaven and earth—with a new Jerusalem—will become the eternal abode of perfect Holiness. In the midst of all the trials and travails of the life we live now, we can find peace and joy by looking forward to a time when we will be in God's presence, worshiping Him.

Let us live our lives looking forward to His coming with great anticipation and joy! Let us lift our heads above the troubles of this life and keep our eyes firmly fixed on the hope of His coming. Then we will be a beacon of hope to the world.

> He who testifies to these things says, "Yes, I am coming quickly." Amen. Come, Lord Jesus. The grace of the Lord Jesus be with all. Amen (Revelation 22:20,21).

Zechariah at a Glance

Theme of Zechariah:

Author:

Historical Setting:

Purpose:

Key Words:

Segment Divisions		Chapter Themes
		1
		2
		3
		4
		5
		6
		7
		8
		9
		10
		11
		12
		13
		14

MALACHI

INTRODUCTION TO MALACHI

Do you want God to open the windows of heaven and pour out blessings upon your life? Is there something you need to know or do to receive God's blessings? Malachi knew the secret. About 2400 years ago, he told the people of Israel how they could secure God's blessing, and that message still speaks to us today. Malachi came to deliver a message of the need for obedience and the wonder of God's love, promising that God would open the windows of heaven in blessing if only His people would heed His message.

Today we hear messages from all quarters offering conflicting images of who God is and what our relationship to Him should be. It seems that we can barely hear His voice amid the clamor of a "gospel" of health and wealth that emphasizes selfish desires and personal gain. Society tells us we deserve more and better, promising that if only we would buy this or that we would be truly happy. God is approached like some sort of cosmic gumball machine: If we put a coin in the slot and turn the handle, we will get the gumball and a prize.

But God isn't like that. Those who have believed the gospel know He is the Father, He is the Master, He is the Lord, and He is the One who loves us and wants to open the windows of blessing for us. But we must love Him, too...with more than just our words!

As you study Malachi, you will learn how to live in a manner pleasing to God. You will learn how to love Him, honor Him, and obey Him. Then, when the blessings come, you will know it was because of His love. Listen to Malachi's message with your heart, and you will learn the keys that unlock God's blessings in your life.

The Blessing of an Acceptable Offering

Have you ever doubted God's love for you? The children of Israel had been through a lot—captivity and exile from their homeland. They needed a reminder that God loved them. But they also needed a reminder about the importance of obedience to God's commands. One area they neglected to be obedient in was worship. They did their own thing.

But from the very beginning, God had made it clear that those who worshiped Him were to do it His way. To approach God, man needed to bring an offering that would be acceptable to Him. What offering is acceptable to God?

DAY ONE

To familiarize yourself with God's message through Malachi, read chapters 1 and 2. As you read, mark any references to the *LORD of hosts*, the *priest*, and *Israel.* This will help you see who Malachi is writing to and what God has to say to them about certain subjects. If you need suggestions for marking, you may want to mark the phrase *LORD of hosts*[1] with a triangle to remind you of the Trinity; color it purple because it is the color of royalty, and fill it with yellow since God is Light. Mark *Israel* with a star of David like this Israel . Mark *priest* with a "P" and color it blue.

DAY TWO

Today, read Malachi 3 and 4, continuing to mark any references to the *LORD of hosts*, the *priests*, and *Israel* as you did yesterday.

DAY THREE

"Malachi" means "my messenger." As you saw from reading through chapter 1, the first verse tells us that what follows is a message from God through Malachi.

Malachi contains key words and phrases that you should mark. To help you remember which words to mark and how to mark them, write the key words on an index card, color code them as you mark them, and then use the card as a bookmark. This will help you keep track of your markings.

Read Malachi 1:1-5, and mark *you say*[2] by underlining the words. (This phrase also appears as *but you say.*[3]*)* Mark *love* with a heart.

Also note who is talking to whom and what they are talking about. You might also briefly note in the margin of your Bible (maybe in pencil) what the issue is—what problem the Lord is addressing. In verses 1-5, what are God's people questioning?

The story of Jacob and Esau is too lengthy to include in this short study, but for a brief review, read Genesis 25:19-34; Hebrews 12:14-17; and Romans 9:10-16. You might want to record what you learn about these men in your notebook.

There is a great lesson for life in these verses, a message about God's love that is relevant for us today. Meditate on that truth. Write it in your notebook or in the margin of your Bible. Or wait until discussion time if you are doing this study with a group.

DAY FOUR

Read Malachi 1:6 and mark *fear*[4] (or *respect*), *despise(d)*[5], and *My name (Your name)*. If you observe the repeated occurances of *priests* and *Israel*, which you marked on Day One, this should show you the change in the audience for this message and the specific topic in these verses. Verses 1-5 were addressed to which group? Now, in verse 6, who is the message for? What was Israel doing in verses 1-5? What are the priests doing in verse 6? As you read verses 7-10, note what the offense is, what the priests say, and what they do.

Now read Malachi 1:7-10 and continue marking *despise(d)*.[5] as in Malachi 1:6, and also mark sacrifice (or *offering*). Choose a different color or marking symbol for each.

You might also make a list of how God reacts to these actions. How does God describe Himself in these verses? One great blessing you can receive from inductive Bible study is to keep a JOURNAL ON GOD—a record of what you learn about God from your study over the years. If you have never done this, you might want to begin one now and add to it daily.

Read Leviticus 22:17-25 and compare it with Malachi 1:6-10. In Leviticus, what does God say is an acceptable offering? In Malachi, what kind of offerings were the priests making? Why would God not accept the priests' offerings in Malachi?

In Malachi 1:6, God says that a son honors his father and a servant his master, and then He asks, "If I am a father, where is My honor?" Is God a Father to Israel and the priests? Read Deuteronomy 32:6 and Isaiah 64:8 to see two examples of what Moses and the prophets say about God being a Father to Israel.

The Hebrew word used in Malachi 1:6 for "master" is the root of the word "Adonai," which is translated "Lord." God asks the priests in Malachi 1:6, "If I am a master, where is My respect?" Read Psalm 136:3, where "Lord" and "Lords" is the same Hebrew word used in Malachi 1:6. He is Lord; He is Master over Israel and the priests.

How were the priests giving neither honor to their Father nor respect to their Master?

DAY FIVE

Read Malachi 1:11-14, marking the key words on your bookmark. Add *profane*[6] *(profaned/profaning)* and *curse.*

Now read Leviticus 22:31-33 and compare it with Malachi 1:11-14. According to Leviticus, disobeying God's commandments profanes His name. In Malachi, what were the priests doing that profaned God's name?

In Malachi 1:11-14, God said His name will be great among the nations and is feared among the nations. "Among the nations" is a phrase that refers to the Gentiles—all peoples other than Israel. Read Psalm 96 (it's only 13 verses long) to see why His name will be great and is feared among the nations. You might find this psalm a good one to read through and make your own prayer of praise to God.

DAY SIX

According to Malachi 1:14, God curses those who break a vow by sacrificing a blemished animal from their flock. Read Numbers 30:1-2 and Deuteronomy 23:21-23, and note what God says about vows.

The Hebrew word for "swindler" in Malachi 1:14 is also used to describe the actions of Joseph's brothers in Genesis 37:13-20; it is used to describe the Midianites' behavior against Israel in Numbers 25:1-9 and the Egyptians' treatment of Israel before the Exodus in Psalm 105:23-26. If you don't know those stories and have time, read these passages. They should give you insight into God's view of the swindler who deals craftily, the one who breaks a vow. Perhaps God's actions in these Scriptures will help you understand God's reaction toward the priests in Malachi 1.

What application can you make to your own life about offerings or sacrifices you might make toward God? In today's culture, we don't sacrifice lambs or other animals, but what principles can you follow?

Identify the main theme or message of the chapter and record it on the MALACHI AT A GLANCE chart at the end of this chapter.

DAY SEVEN

Store in your heart: Malachi 1:2.
Read and discuss: Malachi 1.

QUESTIONS FOR DISCUSSION OR INDIVIDUAL STUDY

- To what large group of people does Malachi deliver God's message? What smaller groups are addressed?

- What problems are addressed? What did God say Israel doubted? What were the priests doing wrong? Do you see any parallels to today?
- What does God say about His name? What does it mean for God's name to be great among the nations?
- How important is it to keep vows?
- Why do we sometimes doubt God's love? What evidence do we have that God loves us?
- What kind of offerings should we bring to the Lord? How does He view anything that is less than our best?
- How are we to esteem God's name? How can we show reverence?
- How can we show that we regard God as our Father and Master?

Thought for the Week

One of the most important things we can learn from Malachi is that God loves us and we should not doubt His love. God loved Israel and demonstrated His love by choosing them. God demonstrated His love for us by sending His Son, Jesus, to die on the cross for us that we might be forgiven of our sins and have eternal life. John 1:12 tells us that Jesus gave those who received Him the right to be called children of God. That makes God our Father, and God loves His children. He wants to bless us.

According to 1 Peter 2:5, we are also priests to God. One of the most important functions of a priest is to offer sacrifices. What kind of sacrifices are we offering to Him? Romans 12:1 tells us we are to offer ourselves as a living sacrifice to God, holy and acceptable. How then, can we fail to keep our vows to Him? Why would we "swindle" Him, knowing that He loves us, He chose us, and He made us into a royal priesthood?

God said that His name would be great among the nations but that the priests were profaning His name. God's name is so important and should be revered. Isaiah said that "a child will be born to us, a son will be given to us; and the government will rest on His shoulders; and His name will be called Wonderful Counselor, Mighty God, Eternal Father, Prince of Peace." This child was Jesus. As a Christian, you carry the name of Christ. Is there anything in your life that would profane His name? What do people learn about Christ by observing your life? Do you reflect Christ in your speech, your actions, your trust, and your confidence?

Commit yourself to never doubting His love for you and never cheating Him of all He is due. Strive to never give any reason for His name to be profaned. Be a faithful child of God and a faithful priest of God. Worship Him in all you do.

THE BLESSING OF KEEPING COVENANT

Sometimes it seems that you can't trust anyone to keep a promise. Disappointment, hurt, and anger often result from broken promises. But standing by our word and keeping our promises bring a positive result—the trust and respect of those to whom the promise was made and those who witness our faithfulness. Don't you want to be found faithful?

In chapter 2 of Malachi, we are introduced to the concept of "covenant."* A covenant is the most solemn, binding agreement anyone can make. It involves promises to and responsibilities toward the covenant partner, as well as consequences for breaking the covenant promises. As we study Malachi, we need to remember that keeping covenant shows reverence for the covenant partner, and breaking covenant profanes both the covenant and the covenant partner's name. There are many covenants in the Bible, but in Malachi 2, two covenants are specifically mentioned and they are the two main subjects of the chapter. Let's examine the responsibilities of the covenant partners and the consequences for failing to keep those responsibilities.

---

* For more in-depth study of "covenant," contact Precept Ministries International at 1-800-763-8280 or visit www.precept.org. Kay Arthur has also written an excellent book on the subject called *Our Covenant God: Learning to Trust Him*, published by Waterbrook Press.

DAY ONE

Read Malachi 2:1-9 and mark the words on your bookmark. Add *covenant* and color it red with a yellow border. You marked *fear* in chapter 1. In chapter 2, the same Hebrew word is translated as *reverence* and *revered.* Mark these two words the same way you marked *fear* in chapter 1. Note who is addressed in these verses—is it still the priests?

Last week, you marked all the references to the priests, and you observed in chapter 1 of Malachi that God was not pleased with the sacrifices the priests were offering. The priests were the sons (descendants) of Aaron. Read the account of God choosing Aaron and his sons to be priests perpetually in Exodus 28:1; 29:9; and 40:13-15. Aaron was a descendant of Levi, one of Jacob's 12 sons. (Read Exodus 6:16-23 if you have time.)

When God chose Aaron and his sons to be priests, there was no mention of covenant. But if you will read Numbers 18:19 and 25:10-13, you will see that God calls the sacrifices of the priesthood a covenant of salt (a covenant of fidelity or loyalty) and calls the priesthood itself a covenant of peace (a covenant of submission).

In Numbers 25, God makes this covenant of peace with Phinehas, the son of Eleazar, the son of Aaron, the descendant of Levi. So the covenant with "Levi" refers to a covenant with whom?

DAY TWO

Read Malachi 2:1-9 again today and make a list of the things that a good priest was to do. Also list what the priests had actually done and note the contrast. You might record these lists like this:

WHAT A PRIEST SHOULD DO	WHAT THE PRIESTS HAD DONE

Reading 1 Peter 2:5,9 and Revelation 1:6 and 20:6 will give you insight into those whom God calls priests today. As you read these verses, note any lessons for life you discern in respect to your responsibilities as a priest.

DAY THREE

Today, read Malachi 2:10-12, marking the words on your bookmark. Add the word *treacherously.*[7]

Note who is being addressed and who has dealt treacherously with whom. What was the act that profaned the covenant of their fathers and the sanctuary of the Lord?

Now read 1 Kings 11:1-13; Ezra 9:2; and Nehemiah 13:23-29. As you read, observe the dire consequences that marrying the daughter of a foreign god would have on the spiritual health of a king, priest, or any other Israelite. Think about the first of the Ten Commandments —"You shall have no other gods before Me." Why do you think God uses the word "treacherously" in Malachi 2?

If we are not Jews and have no temple such as Israel had in the days of Malachi, is it possible for us to profane the sanctuary of the Lord? Read 1 Corinthians 6:18-20; 2 Corinthians 6:16; and 1 Thessalonians 1:9. What does God expect of us?

DAY FOUR

Today, read Malachi 2:13-16 and mark the key words on your bookmark.

Is Malachi 2:13 addressing the priests, or does it refer to all of Israel? What is the charge the Lord brings against them in this paragraph? How is it related to their offerings?

In Malachi 2:10-12, who was dealing "treacherously" with whom? In Malachi 2:13-16, who is dealing "treacherously" with whom?

What is the "covenant" mentioned in Malachi 2:14? Is it the same as earlier in the chapter?

This passage contains one of the best known statements in Malachi: "'For I hate divorce,' says the LORD." Again the word "treacherously" is used. Be sure you mark it and think about the behavior God is describing as "treacherous."

Marriage was established by God in Genesis 2:21-24. These verses are quoted by our Lord in Matthew and Mark as He answered questions about divorce. To understand what Malachi is saying about marriage, read Genesis 2:21-24; Matthew 5:31,32; 19:3-9; Mark 10:2-9; and 1 Corinthians 7:10-16. God's original design for marriage is revealed in these passages. Think about God's plan for marriage according to these verses, and then see what He thinks about divorce.

DAY FIVE

Yesterday, we looked at God's heart toward marriage, reading several cross-references. Those passages also give reasons why divorce was occasionally granted.* God said that he who divorced except for the reason of adultery was committing adultery. Adultery was against the Law. Read Exodus 20:14,17 and Leviticus 20:10. If adultery has already been committed, then divorce does not cause adultery.

You read Matthew 5:31,32 yesterday. Today, read Matthew 5:27-32 to see the full context of the question of divorce. God hates divorce. What is God's heart toward adultery? Read Romans 13:8-10 and see what Paul taught Christians about adultery.

DAY SIX

Malachi 2:17 is the last verse of the chapter, but some think it actually introduces what follows. (Remember that chapter and verse divisions are not inspired!) Read and mark Malachi 2:17, noting the subject by observing "you say." In chapter 1, the people questioned God's love for them. What are they questioning about God in Malachi 2:17?

Is God the God of justice? Read Deuteronomy 32:4,5 for the answer.

Remember that you want to discern the main subject or theme of chapter 2 and record it on the MALACHI AT A GLANCE chart. Sometimes this can be a challenge when a chapter has as many important teachings as this one. One way to find the main theme is to look for key words that are repeated throughout the chapter, not just in one paragraph. Then you can see how each paragraph relates to that central theme.

---

* For more in-depth study of marriage and divorce, *A Marriage Without Regrets* by Kay Arthur is available through Precept Ministries International and Christian bookstores. Call 1-800-763-8280 or visit www.precept.org.

DAY SEVEN

Store in your heart: Malachi 2:16.
Read and discuss: Malachi 2.

QUESTIONS FOR DISCUSSION OR INDIVIDUAL STUDY

- What had the priests done (or not done) that caused God to rebuke them? What were they supposed to do?
- What did God promise would happen to the priests because they disobeyed His commandments?
- How does what God said to the priests about instruction and turning many back from iniquity relate to us? What role do we have in the kingdom of God?
- Why was God displeased about Israel marrying the daughters of foreign gods? How does that relate to us as Christians?
- How can I keep from profaning "the sanctuary," acting treacherously toward God?
- What treachery had Israel committed toward their wives?
- What is God's attitude toward divorce? Why?
- What role does the Spirit of God have in our dealings with our spouse? What does God expect us to do?
- Is marriage a covenant? How does God view covenants?
- Why is divorce so rampant in today's society? What is the effect of divorce on children?

THOUGHT FOR THE WEEK

A covenant is a solemn, binding agreement to be kept until death, the most serious commitment two partners or parties can make. God is a covenant-keeping God. When He makes a promise, He keeps His word. Because He is completely faithful, He cannot lie, nor does He change His mind like a man.

God also views marriage as a covenant promise. His view is that a marriage vow is as solemn and binding as any other covenant promise. Thus, He hates divorce because it is a violation of that covenant. It mars His intention that two should become "one flesh," and that what He has joined together should not be separated.

God doesn't approve of adultery any more than divorce. Adultery is forbidden in the Law. But God never commands divorce because of adultery; He merely permits it. Jesus explained that divorce was granted because of the hardness of hearts.

What is God saying to us? His word in the days of Malachi is no different from His word today. Nothing has changed about God's attitude toward divorce, nor has anything changed about man's attitude. Yet God always reaches out and says, "Return to Me."

The Blessing That Is Coming

The Lord Jesus Christ will soon return to the earth. When He does, He will bring judgment. But He will also bring blessing for those who esteem His name. Will your name be listed among those who fear the Lord and esteem His name?

DAY ONE

Malachi 3:1-6 responds to the charge of Malachi 2:17. Read Malachi 2:17 again and then Malachi 3:1-6, marking the key words on your bookmark. Make a list of the things you learn about "My messenger." Also list what the Lord of hosts will do in the day of His messenger. Who will be judged, and for what will they be judged?

DAY TWO

Read Malachi 3:7-12 and mark the key words and phrases on your bookmark. Be sure to note the subject in verse 7 and then verses 8-12, and observe how they relate. Read Zechariah 1:3-6 and compare.

DAY THREE

Review Malachi 1:6-14 and compare it with Malachi 3:8-12. What were the people doing that displeased God? List what God says He will do if they return to Him and stop robbing Him.

Tithing was part of the Law. Read Numbers 18:21-26, which shows that Israel was to tithe to support the priests and that the priests were also to tithe to the Lord. No one was exempt. Also read Nehemiah 10:37-39. In those days, a great revival broke out in which the people were convicted to obey God's commands regarding tithing.

The New Testament also speaks about giving. Romans 12:8 and 2 Corinthians 9:7 address our attitude toward giving. Also read Philippians 4:15-19 and 2 Corinthians 8:1-15 where God shows us that giving affects not only our relationship with Him but also our relationships with other believers.

DAY FOUR

Today, read Malachi 3:13-18 and mark the key words that you have listed on your bookmark. Again, carefully observe the occurrence of the phrase "you say," as it shows the charge God brings against the people and what they have said against God.

Compare Malachi 3:18 with Malachi 2:17. What attitude do the people seem to display in these two verses?

How do the people in Malachi 3:16-18 differ from those in Malachi 3:13-15? How are they described, and what does God promise them? How does God reward those who fear and serve Him?

According to Malachi 3:17, is there a special day in which the Lord will act on behalf of His people? Is it related to the day mentioned in Malachi 3:2?

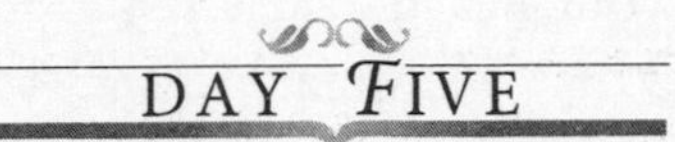

DAY FIVE

Malachi 4 is a continuation of the thought begun in Malachi 3:13. Read Malachi 4:1-6, marking the key words you have listed on your bookmark.

Is "the day" in Malachi 4 related to "the day" in Malachi 3:17?

Make a list of all the things mentioned in Malachi 3:16–4:6 that will happen on "the day."

The word "blessings" is not used in this passage, but are there things that happen on "the day" that are blessings? Read Malachi 3:16 and 4:2 again. Who receives blessing?

DAY SIX

Read Luke 1:5-17 and Matthew 11:2-15 and 17:10-13. Compare these verses with Malachi 4:5,6. Has the prophecy of Malachi 4:5,6 been fulfilled?

List what you learn about those who fear the Lord. Also read all of Malachi again and be sure you make note of the behavior and attitude of those who do not fear the Lord. You might want to make a brief list of these things to remind you of what God has said. Be sure you also understand upon whom the blessing comes and what you need to do to open the windows of blessing.

Finally, record the themes of Malachi 3 and 4 and the overall theme of the book of Malachi on the MALACHI AT A GLANCE chart.

DAY SEVEN

Store in your heart: Malachi 4:2.
Read and discuss: Malachi 3–4.

QUESTIONS FOR DISCUSSION OR INDIVIDUAL STUDY

- Who is coming? When? What will "the day" be like?
- From what you have studied in Malachi, why will "the day" be hard for some?
- What happens to those who do not fear God?
- What happens to those who fear God?
- What have you learned about obedience and blessing?
- Has God spoken to you about areas of your life where you are not walking in obedience?
- How does Israel's example affect us? What lesson can we take for ourselves from God's dealings with Israel?
- Why should we remember the Law of Moses if we are not under the Law?
- How does the messenger of Malachi 3:1 relate to Elijah in Malachi 4:5?

THOUGHT FOR THE WEEK

God, after He spoke long ago to the fathers in the prophets in many portions and in many ways, in these last days has spoken to us in His Son, whom He appointed heir of all things, through whom also He made the world (Hebrews 1:1,2).

Malachi was the last prophet in the Old Testament. After him came 400 years of silence. Then God spoke again in His Son, Jesus, through His life, through His death, through His resurrection, and through the written words of Scripture. Today, if you hear His voice, do not harden your hearts as Israel did in the wilderness. Be sure that the Word preached to you is accepted in faith. Let it take root deep in your soul so that you might be obedient to it. Let it not be said of you that you doubt God's love or rob Him in tithes and offerings, that you neglect the flock by not teaching truth, or that you fail to recognize the value of serving God.

On those who fear God's name, the sun of righteousness will rise with healing in its wings. Let Him open the windows of blessing on you because you love Him and fear Him, because you obey His commandments to show your love and fear. Love the Lord your God with all your heart, and with all your soul, and with all your strength, and with all your mind; and love your neighbor as yourself.

Malachi at a Glance

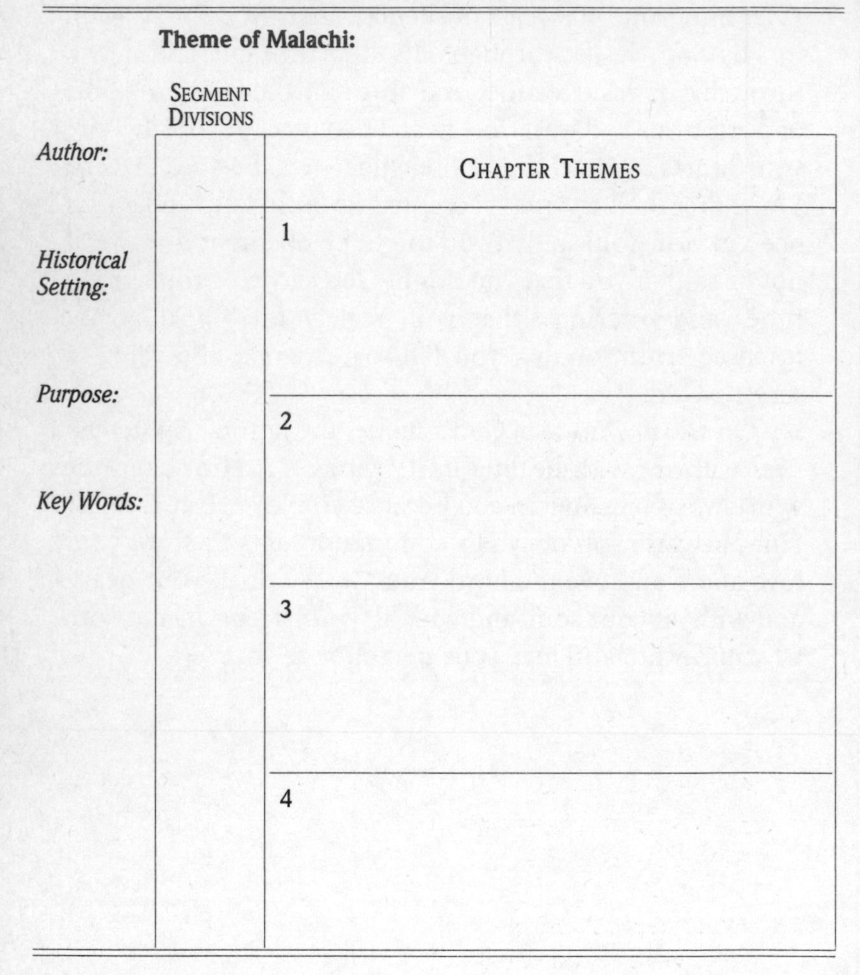

Theme of Malachi:

Segment Divisions	Chapter Themes
	1
	2
	3
	4

Author:

Historical Setting:

Purpose:

Key Words:

Notes

Zechariah

1. NIV: *Lord Almighty*
2. NIV: *return, turn*
   KJV: *return, turn*
   NKJV: *return, turn*
3. NIV: *I had a vision*
4. KJV: *What seest thou?*
5. KJV: *the Lord shewed me*
6. NIV: *I looked up*
   KJV: *lifted I up mine eyes*
   NKJV: *I raised my eyes*
7. KJV: *threescore and ten years*
8. KJV: *heathen, Gentiles, people*
9. NIV: *left*
   KJV: *remaineth*
   NKJV: *remains*

Malachi

1. NIV: *Lord Almighty*
2. NIV: *you ask, by saying*
   KJV: *ye say, ye said, ye have said*
   NKJV: *by saying, you said*
3. NIV: *but you ask*
   KJV: *and ye say, but ye said*
   NKJV: *yet you say, but you say*
4. NIV: *revere*
5. NIV; KJV; NKJV: *contempt(ible)*
6. NIV: *desecrated*
7. NIV: *break (broken) faith*

Books in the New Inductive Study Series

Teach Me Your Ways
Genesis, Exodus, Leviticus, Numbers, Deuteronomy

Choosing Victory, Overcoming Defeat
Joshua, Judges, Ruth

Desiring God's Own Heart
1 & 2 Samuel, 1 Chronicles

Walking Faithfully with God
1 & 2 Kings, 2 Chronicles

Overcoming Fear and Discouragement
Ezra, Nehemiah, Esther

Trusting God in Times of Adversity
Job

God's Blueprint for Bible Prophecy
Daniel

Discovering the God of Second Chances
Jonah, Joel, Amos, Obadiah

Opening the Windows of Blessings
Haggai, Zechariah, Malachi

The Call to Follow Jesus
Luke

The Holy Spirit Unleashed in You
Acts

God's Answers for Relationships and Passions
1 & 2 Corinthians

Free from Bondage God's Way
Galatians, Ephesians

That I May Know Him
Philippians, Colossians

Standing Firm in These Last Days
1 & 2 Thessalonians

Walking in Power, Love, and Discipline
1 & 2 Timothy, Titus

Living with Discernment in the End Times
1 & 2 Peter, Jude

God's Love Alive in You
1, 2, & 3 John, Philemon, James

Behold, Jesus Is Coming!
Revelation